BLACK
CHEROKEE

BLACK CHEROKEE

Rhoan Flowers

THE STREETAUTHOR

Rhoan Flowers' Books
Orleans, Ontario
Canada

ISBN: 978-1-989995-07-5 Soft Cover
ISBN: 978-1-989995-08-2 E-book

Library & Archives of Canada
395 Wellington Street
Ottawa, Ontario
K1A-0N4

Due to the dynamic nature of the Internet, any web addresses or links contained in this book may have changed since publication and may no longer
be valid.

In Commemoration of The
African American Black Indian

Black Indians were people of mixed African American and Native American heritage, who have strong ties to the Native American culture. Many Indigenous people of the Eastern Woodlands, such as the Pequot, Narragansett, Lumbee, and Cherokee, have a significant number of African ancestors. During the days of slavery after Africans were transported to America, several of them escaped and ran great distances to flee from their slave masters. These freedom seekers often came across Indians who were in some cases vicious and intolerable towards other tribes of people, however, a small number of Native Tribes would offer solitude. The similarities between some indigenous Native American and the Traditional African Slave became the bonding factor between the two nations, which led to their union wherein they became one people. Africans were eventually allowed to form marital bonds with the Native Indian, which enabled them to produce offspring that helped to bind the cultures. In todays society only a small percentage of African Americans are descendants of Black Indians, which is a rare breed of people, who will forever honor and celebrate their true heritage.

**

Special Dedication

Ashton S. Williams
Sydney A. Flowers

Thanks To
Book Cover Design

Brittany Wilson

Introduction

The Nevada Cherokee Tribe was the most diverse of all the Indian groups across America, with more than one fifth of its members' being descendants of African Americans. Due to the tribe's unique heritage they kept to themselves and rarely integrated with outsiders to avoid racial confrontations. A wealthy Caucasian male and his gun hands robbed two Indian warriors of a majestic wild stallion, then killed both men in cold blood. The incident sparked tensions between the Caucasians and their Native neighbours, who went on the Warpath to gain justice. The United States Cavalry was sent to settle the uprising and in so doing left the Cherokee Tribe decimated following their battle. Defeated and threatened with extinction the surviving Indians retreated into hiding and disappeared for several years. A pair of unlikely brothers would grow into men, and attempt to right the wrongs of the past, but in so doing, jeopardized the safety of their entire tribe. The cowboys against whom the Indians fought, were intent on exterminating the entire tribe. To accomplish their mission, the cowboys vandalized, and killed innocent settlers to frame the natives, and gained approval for their premeditated plot. For a second time in their history the Nevada Cherokee Tribe went to war against the U.S Cavalry and a band of cowboy bigots. To save their people and themselves, these young warriors must lead an entire tribe of natives to safety, from the clutches of greedy and xenophobic men!

CHAPTER
ONE

Hiroaku and Tusinshi had firm grips on a rope, tied around the neck of a powerful, tussling black stallion. They had managed to capture the alpha horse called Tornado, which belonged to a herd of wild strays that roamed freely about the mid west plains. After chasing the horse for miles, Tusinshi who was far ahead of Hiroaku and Walking Turtle, trapped the animal in a cavern between steep cliffs and lassoed it. With his rope firmly around Tornado's neck, Tusinshi leapt off his horse and tried to control the powerful beast, until Hiroaku arrived to help. The magnificent and stunning animal repeatedly stood on its hind legs, as it railed high in the air and kicked its front legs in opposition. The sun was hot and directly above them in the afternoon sky, so the struggling Indians tried not to fight the horse, and instead waited for it to grow a bit weary then calmed down.

Walking Turtle was the chubbiest of the three and the slowest horse rider, therefore, he got lost during the chase and was unsure where his friends went. As a Native Cherokee his tracking capabilities were deplorable, so instead of continuing straight after he exited some brushes, Walking Turtle turned right, and followed a set of horse tracks he thought were his associates'. Once Tornado began fighting and nickering at the idea of being captured, Walking Turtle adjusted his heading and gravitated towards the noise. Instead of directly

1

ascending on his associates' location, the trailing Indian inexplicably appeared at the top of the right cliff, where he sighted his friends below toiling over the most magnificent horse any of them had ever known. The lost Indian began looking over the cliff's edge for a safe way down, yet was unable to spot a pathway, along which his horse could descend.

"Hiroaku, Tusinshi… I am up here; wait for me I find a way down," Walking Turtle yelled, but his voice fainted beneath the nickering of the horse!

The Alpha Horse fought its hardest to escape, but was up against steep rocks with its only passage being blocked by its antagonists. Tornado began settling down after a lengthy battle, thus, Tusinshi crept closer to the animal and gently rubbed its neck. The young Indian trapper had an astonishing horse whispering talent, which he used to soothe the animal's wild temperament. As a sign of great respect and admiration, Tusinshi withdrew a green apple and fed it to the magnificent horse, which was infamous throughout the lands for leading one of the greatest wild herds. Once Hiroaku observed that the horse's violent rage had subsided and it was indeed safe to move closer to Tornado, he slowly crept in and gentle rubbed his hand against the physically intimidating animal. Tusinshi spoke to Tornado and whispered soothing words to the horse, while he fixed the rope around its neck and prepared to slowly mount the massive stallion.

"You know that I have chased you since I was a little boy, and no one deserves the chance to own you! But if you could be my feet and carry me with you across this land, I will honor and cherish you as long as you stay," Tusinshi whispered into Tornado's ear, before he leapt aboard!

The horse remarkably remained calm despite never having a human on its back. Tusinshi gently rubbed Tornado's neck and patted him on the side which helped to increase the bondage between man and animal. While they bonded five cowboys rode up unexpectedly and blocked in the Indians, who like Tornado before them had nowhere to escape. Walking Turtle was surveying the landscape for an alternative way down, when he saw the cowboys trapped his companions, and quickly moved out of sight. The astonished Indian dismounted his horse, then crept closer to the ledge on his stomach with his Winchester Rifle at hand, where he watched to see what would unfold between his friends and the cowboys.

"Well, I'll be damned! I've heard of you coloured Indians before, but this is the first time I've actually seen one of y'all with my own two eyes," Mr. Jonathan Becket stated, as he leaned forward in his saddle!

"Sure is boss," Quick Draw said!

"I believe you're sitting on my horse boy! Get off," Mr. Becket warned!

"You heard the boss boy! Get down off his horse," repeated Quick Draw!

"This not your horse! He lives free as the wind," Tusinshi argued!

"Boom!" Quick Draw withdrew his holstered pistol and shot Tusinshi directly in the chest. The bullet's impact propelled the coloured Indian off the horse and sent him hurling to the ground.

Hiroaku immediately threw his hands in the air pleading for leniency, but Quick Draw slowly turned his pistol towards him. The other three hired gun hands were not about to let Quick Draw have all the fun and withdrew their weapons. All four employees shot and killed Hiroaku in cold blood, then took time to replace their spent bullets they fired, before they re-holstered their firearms. Walking Turtle could not believe what he had witnessed, so he aimed his rifle at Mr. Becket, and thought about pulling the trigger. Knowing that he would have had to outpace the other cowboys, and how incredibly slow he was on horseback, discouraged Walking Turtle from discharging his weapon. Hence, he instead rolled onto his back and stared up at the sky with tears rolling down the sides of his face.

Ralph, one of the hired guns, rode over to the cornered stallion, grabbed the attached rope, and dragged the animal along. After Mr. Becket and his hired gun hands departed, Walking Turtle made his way down to the bottom of the cliff, where he struggled to come to terms with the killings, but placed his friends onto their horses and brought them back to their village. The Cherokee Indians of Nevada operated differently from their relatives in the state of Georgia and other parts of America, wherein they were against the enslavement of colored people, and chose instead to live in harmony with them. It was dark by the time Walking Turtle rode into their village yelling, 'we must avenge this injustice,' at which a crowd immediately formed and assisted with the bodies!

"What has happened to my son," Hiroaku's mother cried?

"Five white eyes kill them both, then steal their horse," Walking Turtle shouted, as he dismounted his horse and ran off!

News of the killings swooped through the village like a deadly storm, as boisterous mourners hoisted both corpses onto wooden stretchers and brought them to their individual places of residence. Before attending to anything else Walking Turtle made his way to Chief Lakoatah's tent, where three elders were conversing among themselves.

"Chief Lakoatah it is I Walking Turtle," announced the witness who was slightly winded!

"You may enter Walking Turtle son of Setting Moon; tell us what has happened," Chief Lakoatah stated?

"Hiroaku and Tusinshi captured the mighty Tornado! Then five white eyes, killed them, take horse," exclaimed Walking Turtle!

"What white men," angrily enquired the Cherokee Chief?

"They ride toward Jasper," said the Witness!

Chief Lakoatah grew enraged and charged out of the hut to personally inspect the bodies. The elders with whom he spoke accompanied him, knowing the magnitude of whatever was to be the outcome. By the time Walking Turtle finished briefing Chief Lakoatah the entire village was in an uproar over the killings. The deceased warriors were young men who lived with their fiancées, therefore, the corpses were taken to their dwelling and presented to their women. Indians throughout the village had heard about what transpired, so they all went to the widows' huts to offer their condolences. Walking Turtle arrived at his deceased friends' residences, to find mourners weeping and screaming for blood.

Hiroaku and Tusinshi were very close friends who lived adjacent from each other. Hiroaku's fiancée Shushuni had recently given birth to their first son, while Tusinshi's fiancée Darmah, was entering her eighth month of pregnancy. When the mourners brought the dead bodies home, and Darmah saw her unborn son's deceased father, a sharp cramp gripped her stomach, at which she immediately went into labour. That gruesome day turned into a warm summer's night, thus, contrary to the Coyotes howling in the distance, and an outraged mob forming a War Party, Darmah's labour screams was the most prevalent sound throughout the Cherokee Village.

The Cherokee Chief briskly walked up to Hiroaku's covered body, stooped to the ground, and removed the covering. The body was in a deplorable state with more than eight bullet wounds, the worst of which disfigured Hiroaku's face, and left a gaping hole at the back of his head. After inspecting the body, the Chief went over to Tusinshi's corpse and did the same. Chief Lakoatah had tried his best to abstain from engaging in a war versus the White Man, but there was no justification for the theft of the horse, and the killing of two innocent Indians.

After seeing first-hand, the mutilation, Chief Lakoatah stood before his braves and lamented, "many moons passed, since the White Man come to this land. The Indian know these vast lands could be shared, so we welcomed our new neighbors, in peace! But since then, they only try to dominate these lands, and take all for their people! As Indians we only take what we require from these lands, but they show us they have no honor in respecting the land! The White Man choose to disrespect the Cherokee; now the Cherokee shall remove him from our lands!"

"Yeh, yeh, yeh, yeh, yeh," cheered the crowd!

The Cherokee Chief and his vengeful war party members dispersed and returned to their huts, where they retrieved their weapons, and prepared themselves to plunder, by administering war paint to their faces and bodies. The warriors re-emerged from their huts, to find their overzealous chief wearing his War Head Dress, and trotting about atop his horse, with his Winchester Rifle and spear in the opposite hand. Cherokee warriors were excellent horse handlers; therefore, they simply ran up to their saddleless mounts and leapt aboard like stuntmen. Once the War Party got assembled Chief Lakoatah made his way to the front of the group, where he simply lifted his hand in the air, and they galloped away.

The Cherokee Village was located in Nevada ninety miles from the closest town of Jasper, which had the biggest population of outlaws in the western states. The Indians' lived in the Mountain Range of Sierra Nevada, and generally kept to themselves, although they would travel into town twice yearly to trade Fur for supplies. There were three Indians living in the town of Jasper, who made their way doing the demoralizing jobs, that other town folks would reject. Instead of attacking the bigger town, there were a number of settlers living between Jasper and the Cherokee village, who Chief Lakoatah sought to displace, loot, and murder as revenge for both their losses.

Inside Tusinshi's hut located by the edge of the village was his colored fiancée Darmah, who laid on her back with both feet elevated and spread apart. Assisting Darmah with the delivery of her child was her dear friend Shushuni, who had herself given birth to a son only six days prior. A pair of midwives, one an elderly native Indian woman name Syckarie, and a coloured Indian female name Yanique, were also present to provide their valued expertise, having delivered several of the children in the village. Darmah had been in labour since she saw Tusinshi's body nearly an hour prior, however, her child experienced complications exiting the womb. Yanique performed a hand examination, that revealed the Umbilical Cord was wrapped around the child neck. The midwives have only experienced such a predicament once before, and knew that either the mother or child could die during the delivery procedure. Both midwives discussed the situation with Darmah and advised her of what dangers laid ahead. Before the midwives began, Darmah plead with them to 'please save her baby, even at the expense of her life?' The labouring mother then turned and asked Shushuni, 'to raise the child should anything unforeseen happened?'

Without the assistance of modern-day pain relievers, Syckarie and Yanique went to work on Darmah, and successfully delivered her baby boy who was not initially breathing. The ladies passed the child to Shushuni, who immediately cleaned away the mucus, began pumping his heart, and continually blocked his nostrils while she blew oxygen into his mouth. Darmah held on and watched the extensive effort given by her friend, whom she knew was also mourning. After exhausting all her strength, the moment Darmah heard her baby's cry for the first time, her eyes closed for the last.

"Coyote," Darmah whispered with her last breath!

Despite her sorrow, Shushuni was elated for her friend whom she turned towards to pass the baby to, then realized that Darmah had stopped breathing. All the ladies began weeping for their community's lost, as Yanique covered Darmah's body with a blanket. Shushuni lifted the crying baby high above her head and said, "you shall be called Coyote!"

Chapter
TWO

Beth Becket and her husband Jonathan started from a humble beginning, before they moved west from Georgia in hopes of gaining wealth and a better life for their family. They made the trip with their two-year-old son William, who contracted a serious flu and died before they reached their new home. The child's death was excruciatingly difficult for Beth and took a few years for her to get over, but she never relinquished some of his belongings.

Even though people publicly believed that Jonathan was the dominant head of their family, Beth secretly ruled her husband and gave the orders. The disheartened yet ambitious mother opened the first seamstress store in Jasper, where she mended and made new clothes for the locals. Beth began making enough money to import unique fabrics from across the country, which she used to create fabulous dresses for the church attendants.

Several years later the Beckets' had another son whom they named Horace, who was born so tiny and premature, that the doctor doubted he would survive a month. However, the boy would exceed all expectations and grew into a healthy young lad. Both Beth and Jonathan saved enough money to start a small cattle ranch, but she left the strenuous work to her husband, and dealt solely with her seamstress business.

Jonathan Becket became highly successful and expanded their cattle ranch from five acres to eighty-five acres, with over a thousand heads of cattle. Their property was located eight miles away from the town of Jasper, with restrictions posted on the surrounding barbwire fence, prohibiting everything from trespassers to grazing. Mr. Becket had up to twenty men under his employment, from Cattle Ranchers to murdering Gun Hands, and always travelled with a least two armed guards.

Becket became the wealthiest businessman in Jasper, and bought several businesses in town, including Jasper's Hardware Store and Becket's Hotel and Saloon. There were three main structures built on his cattle ranch, the largest of which was his two story, four-bedroom home in which he resided with his wife and son, a large bunk house for his ranch hands, and a stable that housed several types of animals.

Farmers and cattlemen from around the country would often travel to Nevada, to purchase livestock from Becket's herd, which was renowned for quality beef. Jonathan offered customers who wanted their acquisitions delivered to them a contingency plan, where for an additional fee his cattlemen would deliver their animals. Success eventually changed Jonathan, wherein the once mild-mannered individual became brash and arrogant towards others, yet his wife was the sole exception to whom his mannerism never wavered. Beth Becket would have her husband bring her to work and pick her up every evening, which was an uncanny situation for any cowboy.

Jonathan rode into the town of Jasper one evening on a single horse, open back wagon, with four of his hired gunmen on horsebacks trotting alongside him. The sun had just began creeping off to the west and a mild breeze blew across the dry landscape, which made the streets through town very dusty. Three little boys dashed across the street ahead of the wagon pretending they were riding horses, as they pranced about with long pieces of sticks between their legs. A number of town folks walked along the sidewalks with handkerchiefs or some sort of fabric covering their nostrils to avoid the dust. Mr. Becket stopped his wagon in front of the sheriff office, where Ralph took control of the reigns and allowed him to disembark. Both Quick Draw and Mute rode over to a hitching rail, where they dismounted, tied off their horses, and accompanied their boss up to the facility.

"Bobby run tell Beth we'll be along in a minute," Jonathan instructed!

"Yes sir, Boss," Bobby answered!

The gun hand rode off down the street and disappeared after turning onto another road. Mr. Lester who was a very prominent businessman in town, exited the facility and closed the door behind himself.

"When is you gonna sell me that public stable," Mr. Becket asked?

"With all the businesses you already own here in town, you don't want that broken down shack," Mr. Lester joked!

"I'm a businessman Mr. Lester, I know there is a price for everything, would be a pity to see that stable go up in flames," Mr. Becket threatened!

"That might just be the reason I need to build back a better stable! I own the land Mr. Becket; like you, I am a businessman! Evening to you Mister Becket," Mr. Lester answered, before he tipped his hat and walked by!

Mr. Becket knocked the door to the jail and waited until someone awarded him entry, before he walked in. Deputy Eli Marks answered the door with a 12 Gauge Shotgun at hand and allowed the visitors to enter. Jonathan and his associates first looked over at an unconscious male inside a cell, who appeared to have been beaten. Sheriff Brad Hopkins sat behind his desk eating supper with his six shooter, directly ahead of him on the desk. Once Deputy Marks allowed Mr. Becket and his guards entry, he took up position behind them and kept his weapon pointed at their backs.

"Evening Mister Becket, what can I do for you," Sheriff Hopkins stated?

"Enough with the pleasantries sheriff, you already know why I'm in here," Mr. Becket answered!

"Well, if you're here for your drunken birthday celebrating foreman over there in that there cell? He ain't going nowhere until he sobers up and sees the judge about all those damages he caused," Sheriff Hopkins explained!

"I don't care what he did, I want him out now," Mr. Becket argued!

"Unless you got a judge back there in your back pocket, he ain't going no-where! You have a beautiful evening now Mister Becket," Sheriff Hopkins declared.

"You're coming up for re-election soon sheriff! I think you should seriously consider who you offend," Mr. Becket countered!

"I'll leave that decision to the good folks of Jasper sir! You again have a good evening," Sheriff Hopkins answered.

Jonathan Becket and his entourage walked out of the town's jail and climbed aboard their individual transports. Deputy Marks walked out onto the porch with a cigar between his lips, and his shotgun at hand, and engaged in a stare down with Quick Draw. The deputy watched as they all rode away and disappeared from sight, following which he lit his cigar and smoked. Mr. Becket and his guards reached their next destination just in time to catch Beth Becket closing the doors to her seamstress store. Jonathan again dismounted and helped his wife climbed aboard, during which he noticed a thick black smoke and huge flames in the distance.

"Ain't that Puckett's place over yonder," Jonathan enquired?

A man with his cowboy hat almost covering his face aboard a horse came galloping down the road and sped by Jonathan as he mounted his wagon.

"Indians! Savages! Indians," the man yelled!

"There goes Puckett boss," Quick Draw stated!

The man continued down to the end of the road and turned toward the jailhouse. Instead of exiting town in the direction from which the man came, Jonathan curiously turned the wagon and rode back toward the jailhouse. By the time they reached, a huge crowd had gathered with citizens eager to uncover what had transpired. Mister Puckett was on the sidewalk in front of the jail speaking with Sheriff Hopkins and those who gathered, while other interested enthusiasts flocked.

"I went out to check on my traps late this afternoon and got back just a while ago to find them damn Indians murdering my entire family! Look yonder, you can see the smoke and fire from my house burning! I damn near didn't get away neither! But them damn sons a bitches, killed my babies," Mr. Puckett shouted as he wiped away tears from his eyes!

"What kind of Indians was they," asked someone in the crowd?

"I wasn't about to stop and ask em," fired back Mr. Puckett!

Beth looked worriedly at Jonathan as those in attendance became frantic with fear.

"What do we do sheriff," asked another person from the crowd?

"Listen we are all going to have to protect our town! I doubt which ever group of Indians they are, they go attack us, but we won't be taking any chances," Sheriff Hopkins stated.

"Jonathan, what about Horace," Beth exclaimed?

"Let's get out of here boys... Yah," Mr. Becket instructed!

CHAPTER
THREE

Unionville, Nevada

C hief Lakoatah sat atop his horse in the bushes and watched as Gabe Keel exited his cottage and walked to the outhouse. The sun had not yet fully appeared in the sky, but its presence had begun brightening the region, hence Gabe did not require a lantern to see at such an early hour of the morning. The Caucasian male moved rather hastily while holding a pre-rolled cigarette and a stick of matches between his lips, along with his rifle at hand. Gabe was a family man with a wife named Patricia, an eleven-year-old son Simon, and a thirteen-year-old son named Gabriel. The Keel family planted most of their food and lived off the land, with their Labrador Retriever guard dog that sat by the front door, two cows, a pig, and four chickens. Even with the increased lighting the Indians who have been on the warpath for two weeks were completely invisible along the tree ridge, therefore, Gabe felt assured his property was safe, as he latched himself in the toilet.

"Ahhh-Ahhh," loudly groaned Gabe, seconds after his buttocks touched the wooden toilet!

*

Following the loss of their young braves, the Cherokee tribe went on the warpath, where they only briefly returned home to bury the warriors they fought for, and relinquished the items they had stolen. Their laws called for the burial of their citizens on the same day of death or the day thereafter, therefore, their first raids were closer to the town of Jasmin.

Darmah, Tusinshi, and Hiroaku were first washed and scented with Lavender Oil, before their bodies were wrapped in white cotton sheets, with an eagle's feather placed on them, then placed into the coffins. Chief Lakoatah who was also the shaman, performed the prayers and the ceremony amid his mourning community, which lost three young citizens. The burial ceremony for Tusinshi, Hiroaku, and Darmah was an emotional event for the entire tribe, wherein family, friends, and the community wept for their losses. All three bodies were brought onto their burial ground, where they held a touching ceremony, before they were all buried.

Cherokee Indians were allowed a seven-days mourn period, during which the shaman cleansed survivors, cleansed the residence where Darmah died, cleansed their village, and blessed the families of those lost. After seven days of cleansing Chief Lakoatah took the mourners to the river and instructed them to immerse themselves in the water seven times. The mourners had to alternate the direction in which they exited the water with each dip, thus, either facing east or west. After the immersing ceremony, the mourners were presented with fresh clothes, an offering of Tobacco, and sanctified beads, following which they were allowed back into the tribe.

*

Three of the youngest warriors in the War-Party chuckled at the sounds that Gabe made inside the outhouse, until Walking Turtle slapped the disruptor closest to him in the back of the head. There was a total of ninety-three Indian warriors scattered across the woods on horsebacks, twenty-four of which were Coloured Indians who fought in unison with their red skin brothers. They began their rampage across the state with ninety-seven warriors, and have since destroyed twenty-four homes, and killed fifty-two rural settlers. To avoid large causalities, the band of Cherokee Indians abstained from attacking towns with huge populations, and instead terrorized rural homes, stagecoaches, trains, and outposts.

The Indian Chief pointed his finger at Tomack, who slightly tapped his horse with his heels, and commanded the animal to advance, while he selected an arrow from his pouch and armed his bow. Tomack's horse crept softly through the twigs and bushes without him guiding the animal with the reins, which was tied around its neck. The animal brought Tomack closer to the out-

12

house, where he stopped beyond the tree line and awaited Chief Lakoatah's command.

Gabe's guard dog lifted its head and sniffed the surrounding air then barked twice, before it pounced onto its four legs and prolonged the barking. The dog's sudden agitative state startled Gabe, who accidentally burnt himself when he dropped his cigarette on his left leg. Word had already circulated about the Indian's rampage, so fright protruded the rural settler from focusing on the burn, hence, Gabe immediately began peeking through small cracks in the wooden walls, as he grabbed hold of his weapon, stood up, and dragged his Long Johns halfway over his buttocks without wiping himself. Concerned that his Labrador may have detected the raiding savages, Gabe busted through the outhouse's door, and accidentally bumped his foot against a stub, then fell to the ground. Despite injuring his leg, Gabe pounced to his feet and hobbled toward his house with half his clothes hanging on the ground.

Visibility had marginally improved, so Gabe could see the images of Indians along the treeline, as he ran to the safety of his house. The Keels received the warning to evacuate their house days prior, yet assumed the savages would not travel to the northern sections of the state. Their Labrador guard dog had managed to capture the attention of Patricia Keel, who jumped out of bed and ran to the window with an old buck shot rifle. At the sight of her husband running toward their cottage entrance, Patricia started calling out to her two sons as she raced to open the door.

Chief Lakoatah pointed at Tomack, and gave him the order to strike, hence, the young brave took aim and discharged his arrow. The pointy arrow pierced through Gabe's chest from behind and pitched him to the ground, some five feet away from the door. Tomack selected another arrow and shot the barking dog, which ran out from the house toward the treeline, before the animal went silent. The chief waved his hand and signalled a specific group of warriors to attack the cottage, therefore, along the southern section of the residence a group of twelve Indians began circling the house, while they shot out windows and damaged the structure.

"Yeh-yeh-yeh," repeatedly shouted the group of Indians!

Simon and Gabriel awoke to the terrifying war chants of the Cherokee warriors, and crept beside their mother at the doorpost, who stood with the door slightly open while she attempted to encourage her husband. A circling Indian threw his spear at Mrs. Keel and narrowly missed his target, still she remained unfazed and continued calling to Gabe. Both boys saw their father laying face down in the dirt and believed that he was dead, at which they tried to close the door. Gabriel took one final look and realized his father was still alive, when he noticed a slight twitch of the fingers.

"Paw's alive, I'm gonna get him," Gabriel declared!

"No," yelled Patricia!

Despite his mother's objections Gabriel ran out of the house and tried to help his father who was barely breathing. As the young man began lifting Gabe to his feet, a passing Indian fired another arrow into his father's back and killed him instantly. At the realization that his father was dead, Gabriel tried to run back into the house and safely reached the outstretched hands of his mother, before two arrows met their target and plunged into his back. The young man fell in his mother's arms, at which his brother quickly closed the door and picked up the shot gun Patricia had placed on the floor, then moved to a front window. Young Simon Keel rested the weapon on the windowsill and yanked back the hammer like his father taught him, before he took aim and fired at a passing Indian. The bullet blew a young brave clear off his horse and persuaded Chief Lakoatah to reconsider their tactics.

"Tell them burn house," said the Chief!

Once the signal to burn the house was received the circling Indians veered off into the bushes and everything went as calm as it was moments prior. The sudden silence became innerving, as the grieving mother began wondering if the Indians had retreated, or were planning to return? Patricia sat on the floor weeping over her son's dead body, but asked Simon "to look out the window and see what the Indians were planning?" The nervous young lad slowly lifted his head and peeked through the window, and saw the serenity he was accustomed to seeing, which led him to speculate that the intruders had left. Before Patricia could disclaim her son's belief the infamous war cries of the attacking Indians again sounded in their yard, accompanied by the first of several torches through a front window. The torch got caught up in the curtain and sat it ablaze, therefore, Simon grabbed a pale of water and put out the flames.

"Oh my god, they want to burn us out," Patricia nervously yelled!

"Maw your bed is on fire," Simon declared!

Both Keels members ran to the bedroom with towels and tried to put out the fire, but as they fought other sections of their house went up in flames. The Indians continued circling the cottage and ensured that no one escaped, while the thick black smoke inside the residence engulfed everywhere. Patricia and Simon at first covered their noses with pieces of cloth and fought diligently for their lives, but the smoke became unbearable and overwhelmed them. Simon grabbed his mother's hand and attempted to move towards the door to escape, but Patricia feared what would happen to them should they get captured and stopped her son from leaving the surrounding furnace. The smoke eventually rendered them both unconscious, thus, the last surviving Keel members fell victims to the arsonists, and burnt to death inside their home. After they were confident that they had achieved their mission of exterminating another Caucasian family, the gang of Cherokee Indians slowly rode away from the scene.

CHAPTER
FOUR

Geneal Warren Bailey of the Hundred and Fifteenth Cavalry Division, stationed in Las Vegas, Nevada, received a telegram directly from President Donald Jackson. The general paced about his office at the Fort Adams Army Base and read the letter, before he passed it to his Chief Lieutenant Benjamin Dwyer, who was also present. In the letter the U.S President expressed his concerns over the Indian uprising in Nevada and ordered the general to proceed there immediately, and settled the matter diplomatically. If a diplomatic solution could not be reached, the general was instructed 'to use any recommended force necessary and drive the Cherokee back onto their reservation!' While pondering over the letter, Bailey packed his pipe with tobacco and lit it ablaze, then waited for his young lieutenant to comment.

"The president wants us to find out what's got them Indians rattled and settle them down! But from what I've heard about this here uprising general, I don't reckon anyone can settle this diplomatically," Lieutenant Dwyer said!

"That why the president asked me specifically to do this! Because he knows how important this division was in getting the Native Peace Treaty signed. Although if they left it up to me, I would not have given them such a huge piece of land," General Bailey stated!

"We just may have a full-blown war on our hands sir," Lieutenant Dwyer indicated!

"Anything is possible with these Indians lieutenant, we just have to keep them in line and under control," General Bailey declared!

"Any information on the number of Cherokee warrior's sir," Dwyer questioned?

"Reports are there is about two hundred or so of those savages. So prepare that Gatlin for transport, should in case we need it," General Bailey ordered!

"So, when do we leave Sir," Lieutenant Dwyer asked?

"Get the men ready, we leave in a half hour Lieutenant... And Dwyer, send those two Apache scouts in here," General Bailey responded!?

"Yes sir," indicated Dwyer!

Lieutenant Dwyer saluted the general and exited his office. The scouts who General Bailey spoke of were tending to the horses by the barn, hence the lieutenant walked by their direction and instructed them 'to visit with the commander!' Both scouts stopped their chores and went directly to General Bailey's office, where they discussed in full length their mission ahead.

Lieutenant Dwyer walked directly to the officers' barracks and informed his subordinates they would be departing at the time specified to him. After he announced their scheduled departure, Lieutenant Dwyer went to his personal quarters and packed his essentials for the trip, then returned to duty and ensured that all the preparations were implemented. Food for the entire regiment was of the utmost importance, so the Lieutenant ensured that they had sturdy carriages and packed one wagon with the cook's assistance. With the food handled, Benjamin then inspected their artillery and made sure they brought along all they required for combat should they be forced into any dangerous engagements. The troops' inspection was the lieutenant's final preparational duties, therefore, he addressed the men inside their barracks and made sure they brought all their essentials.

There were two hundred and fifty soldiers in the regiment all aligned and prepped for inspection by the time General Bailey walked out onto the compound. The army employed a pair of Apache scouts named Jackal and Sasha, who were considered the best trackers in the entire army. While the other soldiers stood at attention, both scouts dressed in their army issued uniforms stood off towards the side of the alignment. The moment Lieutenant Dwyer saw his commander approaching, he instructed the soldiers 'to stand at attention,' therefore, everyone including both scouts did as command.

General Warren Bailey was a very disciplined commander who expected perfection from the soldiers in his division, so everyone made sure their weapons and uniforms were up to his standards. With everything arranged the General slowly walked along the rows of soldiers and ensured that every soldier in his regiment met his specific criteria. Following the inspections, Warren stood before the squad of soldiers and briefed them on the mission ahead.

"We've been assigned by our Commander and Chief, President Jackson to head deep into Indian territory and put a stop to Chief Lakoatah, and this here war party of his... Now the Cherokee is a smart and effective bunch of savages, who will not hesitate to cut your throats; so, I want y'all to be alert at all times! A lot of you have never been in combat, but this is what you've trained for! Your survival now depends on your ability to follow orders and do your job well! We have official orders to carry out gentlemen; so, mount up!"

General Bailey was the first to mount his horse, followed by the commanders beneath him, then finally their basic soldiers. Once the two hundred-and-forty-four soldiers climbed aboard their horses, and their wagon operators signaled they were set to go, General Bailey led them from Fort Adams on the mission, from which much of them would not return. The general led the cavalry from the base out into the wilderness beyond, where shortly thereafter the scouts rode ahead of the army, and eventually disappeared from the unit. While the troops rode at a modest pace, the scouts galloped away and were not seen again until the army stopped to pitch camp later that evening.

The sun was blasphemous in the sky throughout the day, but the soldiers were prepared for the treacherous weather. They rode for nearly eight hours before they came up on a stream with luscious trees and vegetation nearby, therefore, they decided to camp and spend the night there. The town of Jasper was approximately eleven miles away, so before settling in for the evening, General Bailey, Chief Lieutenant Dwyer, and six soldiers rode into town to speak with the elected officials.

The streets of Jasper were as dead as a doorknob when the army personnel rode into town, but as soon as the residents saw who the visitors were, they came rushing out into the streets. General Bailey and his companions dismounted their horses into the hands of hospitable town folks, who were more than willing to secure their horses and welcomed them.

"Welcome, welcome General! We got word that the army should be handling this here revolt by the Cherokee, and have since been waiting to see you people! By the way, I am Victor Rolley, the mayor of Jasper, and this here is Sheriff Brad Hopkins the lawman here in town," introduced Mayor Rolley, at which they shook hands!

"Pleased to meet you," Sheriff Hopkins stated!

"I'm General Warren Bailey, and this is my second in command Lieutenant Benjamin Dwyer," General Bailey lamented!

Becket's Saloon that often offered the residents of Jasper an entertainment establishment to pass the evenings was closed, however, the operator opened its doors and offered the officials a place to talk. Mayor Rolley showed the general and his second in command into the saloon, where Crowder the barkeep offered them glasses and a bottle of Whiskey. After chugging back two shots of liquor with his Chief Lieutenant and the town's officials, General Bailey felt comfortable enough to begin discussing their intention. As the general spoke, the sound of horse feet trampling toward the establishment sounded outside. Jonathan Becket and five of his hired gunmen rode up to the saloon, dismounted, hitched their horses, then walked into the meeting.

"Mr. Becket," surprisingly exclaimed the mayor, as Jonathan walked in, went behind the bar, and fixed himself a drink!

"May I proceed now, Mr. Rolley," asked General Bailey?

"Don't mind me general, I'm just here to protect my interest," Mr. Becket stated!

"Oh, my apologies general! You sure may continue," declared Mayor Roller.

"I have been instructed by the President to deal with Chief Lakoatah and his war party which has been terrorizing the righteous folks of this here state. At the conclusion of my duties, I shall have to provide a written explanation of what this whole mess was about. Now does any of you have any idea what caused this recent uprising, where we now have these savages killing and plundering innocent folks' homes," General Bailey enquired?

Jonathan Becket and his band of murderers looked around the room at the people inside, those standing in the door post, and those who looked in through the windows. The story of what infused the Indians to violence was by then well known throughout the small town, yet still, everyone bit their tongues and remained silent.

"Does anyone know where these Indians were last spotted," Lieutenant Dwyer asked, but again everyone stayed silent?

"Well until we catch up to these scavengers keep your doors bolted shut, and board up those windows closed tight! You never know where those bastards are going to pop up next," instructed the General before they took their leave!

CHAPTER
FIVE

A stagecoach carrying five passengers inside its cabin, with the two operators seated in the box, travelled along their assigned routine route. While Red the driver handled the reigns, his shotgun Kenny carried a Smith & Weston, Winchester Rifle, and kept a constant lookout for Indians and bandits. There was a married couple, two other men, and one other female seated inside the coach, which was destined for Seattle. The Cherokee threat along the Western Celerity Wagon Trail, had driven the basic price for stagecoach seats beyond reason, therefore, ticket sellers charged up to three times the regular fare. Prior to the Cherokee revolt it was customary for one driver to safely maneuver his stagecoach from California to the State of Washington, thus, the increased ticket fares went toward the hiring of private guards. The warring Indians crippled the travelling industry across the west as most Brother Whips either serviced other routes or found other means of employment.

The Beckford Gang intended to stick up the afternoon's stagecoach and kill everyone onboard, after they stole their valuables. The murderous gang, ran by Dave Beckford, plotted to create the illusion that the Indians committed the injustice, while they safely made away with their earnings. There were four other members of the Beckford Gang, one of which was Dave's younger brother Izaiah, their cousin Dimitri, and the Bluff twins Alexander and Marcus. To mimic the Indians, Marcus brought along three eagle feathers, hence, he stuck one in the back of his hair, and passed the other two off to Alexander and Dimitri. All five bandits were wanted for robbing a bank down in Texas, where they made away with over twenty thousand dollars and killed four people during the process. The thieves covered their faces with Bandanas and hid in some bushes, then waited for the stagecoach to appear along the trail, at which they administered pursuit.

The stagecoach was travelling at a modest speed when Kenny sighted Dave and his associates riding toward them. Even though the coach handlers considered the Indians their biggest threat, any, and all disturbances were to be met with excessive force, therefore, Red lashed the horses with the reigns and increased their speed. Kenny fired two shots at the pursuing robbers, before he knocked on the roof of the coach to attract their passengers' attention.

"We got a bunch a bandits on our trail," Kenny yelled, at which the men inside the coach started shooting through the windows at the pursuing thieves!

The violent chase continued for more than four miles with both parties exchanging bullets. Neither the stagecoach handlers nor the bandits had any knowledge that during their shootout chase, the Cherokee Indians were atop the ridge above the valley, watching the altercation with intent to intervene. Members of the Beckford gang failed to maneuver closer to the stagecoach, due to the barrage of weapons being discharged onboard.

With the stagecoach`s four hitches galloping at their maximum speed, the right front wheel fell into a ditch and broke the axle, following which the cabin slammed into the ground. At the high rated speed with which they traveled, both operators on the box got thrown from their seat, as the coach flipped twice before it came to a complete stop. The singletree detached from the stagecoach when it initially slammed into the ground and freed all four horses, which were incredibly fortunate they were not seriously injured.

The stagecoach landed on the left side of the car and left everyone inside a bit disorientated, after such a horrific crash. With the passengers all smudged together it became somewhat of a challenge for them to quickly detach themselves without defiling each other. Two of the male travellers who had been assisting with keeping the bandits at bey, slowly regained consciousness, yet immediately began searching about the floor for their weapons. During the accident, the married female went headfirst into the adjacent seat and broke her neck as a result. While regaining control of his faculties, the husband realized he had fallen on top of her and tried to get off her. When his wife failed to respond both vocally and physically the man checked her pulse, at which he learnt that she had been killed. Instead of retrieving his weapon and helping the other passengers, the husband crouched up in a corner with his dead wife and held her tight in his arms.

Kenny fell a few feet away from his Winchester Rifle, but broke his back, and could hardly move. He could hear the sound of the bandits' horses getting closer and tried to draw his side pistol from the holster. The excruciating pain prevented Kenny from quickly extracting his weapon, therefore, Dave came along and fired two shots into the security's chest. Red had broken several bones in his body and could not move a muscle, nevertheless, Dave inexplicably shot him twice in the chest. To abstain from prolonging the shootout between the passengers and themselves, all the gang members continuously circled the coach, while they filled it with bullets. Once Dave felt satisfied, they had blasted enough bullets into the cabin, he ordered them 'to stop shooting,' and sent Dimitri in to investigate if all the passengers were dead. Regardless of the state of the stagecoach, Dimitri slowly crept in with his weapon cocked to fire, but only managed to confirm what they all had suspected.

Chief Lakoatah and the members of his war party stood atop the hill and watched the entire massacre unfold. While the Beckford Gang searched and ransacked the passengers' belongings, the Chief instructed several of his warriors to engage. Thirty scalp hunting Indians descended from their viewpoint, then charged at the unsuspecting thieves, who did not expect anyone to be within fifty miles of their location. The Indian Chief and the rest of his braves he withheld, watched the incident unfolded from a distance, as the warriors he dispatched unknowingly approached the cowboys. The attacking Indians waited until they were approximately forty yards away from the robbers, before they began shouting their infamous war cry.

"Yeh, yeh, yeh…," repeated shouted the Indians!

"Indians," shouted Izaiah as he ran to his horse and leapt aboard!

Marcus Bluff was inside the cabin going through the pockets, wallets, and purses of the deceased passengers. Dave and Dimitri immediately abandoned their other gang associates and ran to their mounts, climbed aboard, then whipped the horses like jockeys trying to achieve top speed. Alexander Bluff who could not abandon his twin brother maneuvered towards the rear of the stagecoach and began shooting at the Indians. Marcus Bluff had no alternative but to sneak an occasional peek through the opening, as he discharged his six-shooter at their antagonists. With little spacing with which to maneuver, Marcus thought he was in an awful predicament and tried to leap from inside the car. The moment Marcus exposed himself, three Indians tagged him with arrows, at which he died slumped over on the wagon. Alexander managed to shoot one of the Indians off his horse, but his luck then ran out when his weapon needed reloading, and he ducked behind the stagecoach to reinsert bullets. An Indian brave targeted the outlaw as they circled the stagecoach and shot him first in the gut. The pursuing Cherokee then shot Alexander directly in the chest, at which the bandit grabbed hold of the arrow and slowly crashed to the ground. The gang of Indians chased after Dave, Izaiah, and Dimitri, who all abandoned their profits from their foul deeds and rode like horse jock-

21

eys to save their lives.

"I knew this was a bad idea," Dimitri commented!

"You better shut your mouth, before I shut it for you," Dave lamented before he looked back and fired a shot at their pursuers!

"I meant no disrespect cousin," responded Dimitri before he fired a shot at the trailing Indians!

Izaiah who was a few paces ahead of Dave and Dimitri, unexpectedly yanked his reins and brought his horse to a sudden halt, at which the animal riled high into the air on its hind legs. The thief attempting to escape was tossed from his saddle and landed hard on his back, after he was forced to brake by Chief Lakoatah and the remainder of his warriors. While watching his Indian braves moved into position, it became evident where the outlaws might be able escape, therefore, the chief led his followers to intercept them. Once Dave realized they were trapped, he quickly warned his brother and cousin to put away their weapons, with aspirations of reasoning with a race of people they classified as illiterate.

"Now I know how this may look, but it's not as things seem," Dave exclaimed, as he used both hands to signal for calm!

"Now the White Eye, try to become like the Cherokee," Lakoatah joked!

Chief Lakoatah pointed at the eagle feather to his braves, at which they all began laughing and cheering loudly. Dimitri who was already nervous on edge, grabbed for his pistol from his holster, but failed to aim at an adversary, when a warrior threw an axe into his back. With such increased pressure, Izaiah and Dave followed their cousin's lead and went for their guns, thus, the Indians shot them out their saddles.

CHAPTER
SIX

For protective purpose, the Cherokee posted two separate lookouts at elevated positions along the trail that led into their village. During the daytime period, the Indians used either smoke signals or reflective objects to shine the light of the sun as warning messages, to their distant comrades until those in the village were made aware of the visitors. Their village was much easily accessed during the nights, when their security precautions were not in place.

The Apache scouts who worked for the U.S Army wanted the white men to extinguish the entire Cherokee colony. Both scouts expected their Cherokee rivals to appoint at least one lookout, and wanted their allies to march in undetected, therefore, they left camp long before the soldiers. The Cherokee's first lookout was a nineteen-year-old young warrior, who was stationed atop a cliff ten miles away from the village. The young lookout could see for great distances, in every direction, and was instructed to keep himself hidden atop the cliff, then used a shiny object to send the first reflective warning, whenever he saw danger.

While approaching the Cherokee territory, the Apache scouts used their strategic intellect to decipher on which elevated land-space they believed the lookouts would be positioned. They then used their military assigned binoculars and slowly check the cliffs and hillsides, to locate the lookouts they knew would be posted. The Cherokee had their lookouts stationed more than a mile apart from each other, therefore, the first guard was supposed to reflect a signal to the second lookout, who would then light a fire and send a smoke signal to warn the villagers. The Apache scouts cautiously surveyed the high elevation mountains, until they spotted the first lookout, who gave away his location when he adjusted the blanket, he used to shelter himself from the sun.

Once the scouts identified where a lookout was, the Indians removed their army uniforms, allowed their long flowing hair to dangle, and exposed their tribal accessories, to make themselves looked like Cherokee. Both scouts then kept their heads lowered while they rode towards the village, with a modest pace which would not alert the lookout. The young lookout noticed the riders approaching along the plains, yet became less interested in their identities once he noticed they were Indians. While the lookout went back to his relaxing position, the scouts rode by the base of his cliff, where one of them leapt from his horse, then climbed to the top of the hill. The lookout heard the horses' hooves trotted by below and gave them no further attention, after he had assumed the scouts were Cherokee.

The U.S Army scout climbed up to the lookout's position, withdrew his knife, then crept closer to his target. As he moved in for the kill, the scout accidentally unearthed some small rocks, which rolled along the cliff, and startled the lookout. The Cherokee rose from his station and began tussling with the Apache, who tried to plunge his knife into the lookout. Both men fell to the ground and rolled close to the ledge, where the Apache finally gained the upper hand and stabbed his target in the gut. With the first lookout terminated, the scout climbed back down the cliff, where his companion met him with his horse.

The second lookout took notice of the scouts moments later as they rode toward him, across the desert like plains. Even though the riders were Indians, the lookout wondered why his associate neglected to alert him about them, hence, he watched them as the approached. The lookout thought the Indians were returning with news of their ongoing raids, so he stood up, raised his rifle above his head, and began shouting at them. Neither of the scouts waved or responded to the lookout, who thought the riders seemed strange, and moved closer to the ledge to watch them go by. Instead of completely ignoring the scouts as they passed below, the lookout went to the ledge and began watching to identify the riders. Knowing the village was in proximity, the scouts had to eliminate the last lookout for their army companions to freely ride in.

When the scouts reached the base of the cliff and dismounted their horses, the lookout realized they were of another tribe, and fired three shots at them with his Winchester Rifle. The scouts at first had to shield themselves behind boulders, before they returned fire, then began climbing to the top of the slope. The lookout ran to his warning firewood and began gashing the rocks together to create the fire, which sparked seconds later and caught ablaze. Once the wood was fully engulfed, the Indian scattered it to create more smoke, then used a plain sheet to ascend his warning signal. While alerting his people of the danger, the Apache scouts climbed to the top of the short mountain and shot him twice in the back.

With many of the braves away on assignment, their village was less safe, however, they were never completely defenseless. Despite the Cherokee's war party terrorizing settlers across the state, many of their warriors did not partake in the raids, and instead stayed behind. It was primarily the men's duty to protect the women and children, plus hunt to feed the villagers, even though the women were beyond capable of managing such tasks. There were some young boys playing around in the village, when one of them noticed the smoke signal, at which they all began racing home while they sound the alarm. When word of 'intruders approaching' got announced, the villagers immediately dropped whatever activities they were involved in, and either fled into the woods with their children, or armed themselves with spears, knives, bows and arrows, and the few rifle left.

General Warren Bailey led two-hundred-and-thirty-eight soldiers from his battalion into the Nevada Cherokee Indian village, where some of the younger boys were less hospitable. As the soldiers rode into their village, the boys hid behind some of the Teepees and used their Slingshots to shoot some of the soldiers with small stones. Both Apache scouts had reintegrated into the regiment, to defuse any acts of hostility the Cherokee would wish to invoke upon them.

The ride into the village was relatively calm, until the soldiers reached halfway into the camp, where some of females and males formed a blockade. Chief Lakoatah's wife stood ahead of a group of forty-three females, males, and elderly residents who were all prepared to defend their homes. As the cavalry approached, some of the villagers released a huge war cry denouncing their entry, thus, General Bailey brought his soldiers to a halt. After a few seconds of deliberation Chief Lieutenant Benjamin Dwyer rode ahead of the regiment and addressed the local Indians.

"This here is General Warren Bailey of the United States army; and he has been assigned to bring Chief Lakoatah, and this here war party of his to justice! Now if any of you know where to find the chief, you are obliged to surrender that information at once," Lieutenant Dwyer declared!

None of the Indians answered or flinched, as if they were intimidated or concerned, therein, the Lieutenant rode back to his commander and engaged in a brief consult. Both senior ranked officers spoke for a few seconds, during which the commander issued his orders and advised Lieutenant Dwyer how to proceed. With his new instructions the lieutenant rode back to address the Cherokee gatherers, who refused to allow the soldiers any further into their village.

"Does any of you know why Chief Lakoatah is attacking these farms…? The General gotta file a report after this is all done, so somebody better talk up," continued the Lieutenant!

Again, everyone bit their tongues and remained silent. The lack of communication frustrated Lieutenant Dwyer, who turned to return to his commander when Chief Lakoatah's wife Shiloh shouted.

"Rich white man from Jasper, steal horse, kill two young braves! What you do bout that?"

"Even if that were true, that don't give no Indian no consent to shoot white settlers! Now I ask you again, where is Chief Lakoatah," Lieutenant Dwyer stated?

"The chief no here," Shiloh answered!

"You take me for a fool," Dwyer demanded!? "Soldiers, search this entire village!"

At the lieutenant's command, many of the soldiers broke formation and began riding throughout the camp, where they searched every tent. The soldiers found no sign of Chief Lakoatah, therefore, they returned and got back into formation.

"You people are lucky I don't charge everyone of you with conspiracy! We will not tolerate the killing of white settlers by you people; so, whether or not you warn the chief, we will find them, and put an end to their war party!"

With that General Bailey turned his troops around and rode peacefully out of the Cherokee Village. The Apache scouts were extremely disappointed with their commander's decision to leave without massacring the remaining Indians. Even though the villagers with their primitive weapons stood no chance versus the cavalry, they stood their ground and illustrated they would always be a force to be reckoned with. Shiloh waited until the army unit had left, then summoned her youngest son Nyah, and gave him a direct message to transmit to his father. The young brave ran to his horse and leapt aboard like a trained professional, before he galloped away in the opposite direction from the U.S Cavalry.

*

The War Party left a wake of destruction wherever they went, but tracking them was a difficult task with their vast knowledge of the territory. After another two days of searching for the Indian Chief and his warriors, General Bailey's scouts found fresh horse tracks west of Crescent Valley, which indicated the war party was travelling northbound. Estimations by the trackers suggested the Indians were at lease three hours ahead of the army, therefore, they buckled down and rode long and hard to close the gap and reach their assignments. During their search, the soldiers came across many burnt out homes, but in a few instances as a sign of respect, General Bailey had to assign a few soldiers to bury the deceased.

The last torched residence the soldiers came across, sickened many of the troops, when they found the husband for the family nailed to his barn by arrows. The soldiers considered the killing cruel and unjust, after the Indians stapled the man to the boards through palms, and hands. All signs indicated that the other family members were burnt alive, therefore, the soldiers wanted justice. The army scouts inspected the tracks and the burnt cottage, then speculated the Cherokee war party was approximately an hours and twenty minutes ahead of them. After riding hard for hours, General Bailey decided to camp for the night, with the belief they would catch the Cherokee warriors the following day.

*

The cross-country train that travelled across America's heartland was heading eastbound toward the Carolinas, with both passengers and industrial products on board. Transportation managers for the railroad were forced to employ security personnel for trains servicing the Nevada region, due to the Cherokee Indian's uprising. Prior to the hiring, a debate was raised on how many riflemen would be necessary to secure each train, and instead of a dozen plus men per car, the decision was made to appoint two shooters to each passenger's coach. The train had a total of six cars, the first being the engine compartment, two cars transporting passengers, a dining coach, and two boxcars carrying industrial materials, therefore, there were only four security guards on board.

Chief Lakoatah and the members of his war party planned on hijacking the morning train, killed the passengers, and plundered through the cargo. They had attacked one other train a week prior with a less complexed strategy, where they rode alongside the locomotive and killed a few travellers. The group sustained their biggest loss of the campaign thus far, with seven warriors killed, therefore, they looked to incorporate a different scheme which they believed would be more effective. The Indians saw that each locomotive had to stop for water at a refilling station in the middle of nowhere, therefore, they planned on boarding the metal wheel steamroller to execute their plan.

As the train pulled into the refilling station, the armed guards aboard were the first to dismount, and ensured the area was secure, before they began taking on water. The armed guards remained focused throughout the water refilling process, before they climbed back onboard, once the 'all aboard' warning was given! The Indians expected to board the train were all positioned along both sides of the tracks, beginning five yards away from the water container. The Cherokee warriors arrived earlier, dug individual shallow graves, and hid their warriors beneath straw mats, on which they sprinkled soil to provide an authentic look. Each warrior was provided with a piece of unclogged bamboo, that enabled them to breath while submerged. The Indians knew that the locomotives took off extremely slow, before they gradually increased their speed, so they had ample time to climb aboard after the train departed.

The Indians' plans worked to perfection, when none of the cowboys noticed any difference along the plains. As a result, the twenty warriors selected to board, emerged from their shallow graves once they sensed the train departing. Each warrior then ran along with the train, before they unknowingly climbed aboard. All the guards and train operators had returned to the warmth of the interior cabins, so nobody noticed the uninvited intruders.

The Cherokee Chief and his other warriors were five miles ahead awaiting the train's arrival, with the horses belonging to those who boarded. A total of thirteen red skinned and seven dark colored Indians, crept along the roof and sides of the locomotive, as they made their way to their assignments. The two boxcars the Indians leapt onto were at the back of the train, and fortunately for them were not transporting anything dangerous. The rear boxcar was an open top container carrying coal, contrary to the first container, that had multiple compartments with sheep and goats. There were no employees or passengers on either railcar, therefore, the Indians moved about freely inspecting portions of the train.

The first of the two security guards on the rear passenger coach car, was smoking a cigar outside on the porch between railcars with another male passenger. To execute both men without alarming anyone, a pair of warriors from atop the train, armed their Bow and Arrows and synchronized their timing. The Shooters were aware that some cowboys were quick on the draw, therefore, they would only get one opportunity, and a split second to hit their targets. Once the execute signal was given, both warriors pounced into shooting positions and fired their arrows, but only one of the two marksmen was detrimental. The guard got shot in the upper right shoulder and tried retrieving his pistol with the same hand, however, a third warrior hanging from the side of the train, grabbed him from behind by his shirt collar, and pulled him backwards over the guardrail. With the guard and the male passenger overboard, the Indians continued moving.

The group of African American Indians were given a specific task, where they climbed down onto the porch, and joined together on the ramp. The coloured warriors paused by the door, threw their rifles over their shoulders, and instead selected their primitive weapons, such as knives, and axes. Once they were ready to proceed, the leader at the helm opened the door, at which they all ran into the Dining Car like a band of ninjas. There were three employees, a couples seated around a table having breakfast, and three cowboys by the bar inside the cabin. The first person killed was the bartender behind the bar, who started yelling 'Indians' once he observed the attackers, but a knife through the throat silenced him instantly. Before any of the alcohol drinkers by the bar could reach for their weapons, each cowboy received an ax, and thus crumbled to the ground as a result.

Cyndi the waitress, was standing beside the couple's table pouring the man coffee, when the Indians broke in. Hence, she accidentally threw the pot of hot coffee on her customer, as she tried to run to the opposite end of the car. The burnt customer jumped up in discomfort and yelled out in pain, which earned him an axe to the stomach. The waitress failed to reach the door and was knocked to the ground with an ax directly to her back. The second waitress was cleaning utensils and froze with fear, and thus allowed an Indian to walk up and slit her throat. The wife had no idea Indians had boarded the train, until she saw her husband standing with the axe in his chest, before he tumbled backwards. As the waitress grabbed for her neck and fell to the floor, she could hear a faint scream from the female eating breakfast, who got stabbed in the back when she rose from her chair. All the assassins went and recovered their axes and blades, wiped them clean on their victims, then moved to their next assignment.

The Indians expected defiance from the armed cowboys aboard the passenger coaches, therefore, they conjured up a strategy where they divided into teams. While some of the Indians positioned themselves by the exits, others climbed along the roof of both cars and waited to unleash their attack. The Indians on the roof, tied their feet to the guard rails welded on top of the train, then readied their bows and arrows to strike. Once everyone got into position, the Indians outside burst into the passengers' cars through the available entrance and began killing everyone in sight. With the cowboys concentrated on the Indians by the exits, several warriors lunged over both sides of the train, broke in the windows, and fired their arrows at the opponents.

Many passengers who sat close to the windows suffered lacerations to their faces and other exposed areas, when the rooftop Indians stumped in the glass windows. Despite their firearms, the cowboys were dangerously outmatched, nevertheless, some of them stooped between the seats and returned fire at the invading Indians. Immediately following the windows shattering and launching of arrows, some of the warriors untied themselves, and climbed into the passenger carriages. Many of the defensive cowboys crouched between the seats were killed by the window intruders. The Indians caught the cowboys by surprise and were able to get close to their oppressors, wherein, as superior hand to hand combat fighters they slaughtered every white man and woman.

As the train drew closer to the awaiting Indians, the chief signalled his warriors, who exited their hiding place, and began riding towards the locomotive. The conductor inside the engine compartment looked through the window and saw the invaders rapidly approaching the train, so he immediately sounded the warning whistle to alert the onboard guards of the threat. To avoid getting shot by the swarming horsemen, the technician stooped low, closed the compartment door, and increased the train's speed to put some distance between them. There was a small window behind the engineer through which he could check the status of his train, but the thought that they had gotten boarded never crossed his mind. Mata, a colored Indian provided with the task of killing the train's operator, snuck close to the door, and gently opened it. The technician inside the compartment was unarmed and threw his hands into the air, nevertheless, the Indian shot and killed him.

The passenger coaches were littered with the blood of the travellers, thus, several Indians took pleasure in scalping their victims, while others ransacked the carriages. Mata made his way into the operator's compartment and was bewildered by the different knobs and levers, so he had no clue how to stop the train. With the locomotive failing to reduce speed, Chief Lakoatah figured his colored warrior was killed or overwhelmed, so he galloped closer to the locomotive, and leapt aboard the steamroller. Chief Lakoatah's devoted horse continued riding alongside the train, to offer support for its master. The chief unhesitantly moved toward the engine, where he found his confused warrior and applied the braking mechanism, that brought the train to a screeching halt. The Indians were elated by their accomplishment and could be heard cheering all throughout the train.

General Bailey and his troops broke camp at 3:30 that morning, to close the distance and catch the menacing Cherokee War Party. For the first few hours the Apache scouts used torches to follow the Cherokees' horse prints, until the light of the sun made the tracks more visible. The trackers found where the Cherokee camped the previous night at about 5:40 AM, then determined they had missed them by only half an hour, after they inspected the extinguished log wood. The U.S cavalrymen continued pursuit and were within ten miles of the train hijacking, when they began hearing faint sounds of gunshots. Once General Bailey determined that the bangs they heard were indeed gunfire, he instructed his soldiers 'to prepare for confrontation,' before they galloped toward the altercation. The cavalry rode up to a landing along the northeastern section of the train, where they obtained a clear view of the hijacking as it unfolded, hence, General Bailey commanded the Bugle Blower to 'sound the charge!'

"Ta-nap, ta-nap, ta-nap, ta-nah," sounded the Bugle!

The soldiers rode toward the marauders, who were initially unaware of the attackers, until the bugle sounded. The horse handlers were the first to shoot at the cavalrymen, while they attempted to bring their comrades their horses. Chief Lakoatah was still aboard the engine, but jumped onto his horse, and began shouting instructions at his warriors. The Cherokee Chief and his braves on horsebacks tried to hinder the approaching soldiers, to award their comrades inside the coaches, sufficient time to mount their horses to escape. Lakoatah and his horsemen pretended they were heading directly into a clash with a blaze of gunfire, which forced the cavalrymen to yield and return fire. Participants from both parties fell from their horses, as both groups lost braves.

Once the soldiers yielded their direct assault, the Cherokee warriors turned back and rode behind the train. During their brief confrontation, Chief Lakoatah got shot in the left shoulder, and almost fell off his horse, but managed to ride back to safety with the help of his braves. It was impossible for all the train jumpers to safely reach their horses, therefore, the unfortunate warriors positioned themselves inside the railcars, and kept the soldiers at a distance with their sharpshooting. To lessen the loss of his troops, General Bailey stopped at a modest distance from his opponents, and ordered the driver of the wagon that carried his secret weapon, 'to ride to the frontline!'

The driver of the wagon safely swerved the buggy ahead of the troops, and was about to leap from the box into the wagon, when an Indian shot him. Lieutenant Dwyer saw what happened to their Gunnery Private and rode to the wagon, despite being shot at by the Indians. The decision was made by some of the warriors in Chief Lakoatah's entourage, to escape with their injured leader, therefore, they used the train as a shield and rode away. Dwyer climbed aboard the wagon and unwrapped the tarp from around a Gatlin Submachine Gun, before he yanked back the selector lever, and squeezed the trigger. The Indians inside the coaches had the soldiers at a disadvantage, and were controlling the battlefield, until the barrel spinning Gatlin began shifting the tides. Contrary to the other weapons being exhausted on the battlefield, the submachine fired rapidly and dispersed Fifty Calibre Bullets that tore through the train's siding. At the eruption of the Gatlin enforcer, every Indian who should have lowered their heads instead of continuing to revolt, got killed instantly.

With the Gatlin gun supressing the Indians' weapons aboard the train, General Bailey gave the order for other soldiers to circle the locomotive and end the conflict. There were still a few warriors on the opposite side of the train, who hid behind the metal wheels and continued defying the soldiers. Two groups of cavalrymen converged on the train from the engine compartment and the rear boxcar, where they killed whoever was still left alive. At the realization that most of the Indians were attempting to escape, General Bailey and his troops continued pursuit. The general was enraged by the sight of those mutilated on the train and wanted to terminate the war party, so the cavalrymen all rode on without providing the train victims any compassion.

The shootout gave Chief Lakoatah and his escaping warriors some time to put a bit of distance between the U.S soldiers and themselves. Even though the soldiers' horses were extremely exhausted, Bailey and his troops pressed on as they tried to keep up with the Indians. The Cherokee were intelligent people, who knew how to outsmart trackers, but the two U.S Apache scouts were the best they ever faced. Each group rode for miles before the Indians reached a river, where they were slightly beyond the soldiers' view. The Cherokee warriors had to get their injured chief away from the soldiers, who would have certainly thrown him in prison.

To trick the scouts, fifty-five warriors including Lakoatah began riding upstream, while seventeen of their comrades began heading downstream. While Chief Lakoatah and most of his entourage pressed on, eight of his warriors dismounted their horses, and gave the reigns to one of their associates, who rode ahead with their mounts. The eight Cherokee warriors quickly broke branches from a tree and used them to erase the horse prints from the sand for a few yards, before they climbed back onto their mounts and continued upstream.

When the U.S cavalry reached the river the two scouts first checked the other bank, where they found no signs that the Cherokee went that direction. Both trackers then separated where one Apache went slightly upstream and the other walked a bit down stream.

"I find tracks, they go this way," one scout said!

The second Apache scout did not see any tracks as he walked along the riverbed, before he unexpectedly shouted, "I think some of them go that way General!"

"Dwyer take some of the men and head upstream; see if they really went that way! I'll head downstream for a couple miles, then find somewhere to pitch camp till y'all catch up," General Bailey instructed!

"Yes, Sir General! I need fifty a you soldiers with me, and I'll take you Apache, now fall in," Dwyer commanded!

With Chief Lakoatah becoming increasingly weaker, the band of Indians knew they had to get rid of the protruding soldiers. Their chief needed to rest and have the bullet removed from his shoulder, for him to recover and regain his strength. Realizing the urgency, the three-dark skinned and two red skinned Cherokee warriors to the rear of the group, stopped, and made their comrades continued without them. The five warriors came across an area which they thought would be perfect for an ambush, so they released their horses, ran up along the hillside, and hid among some huge boulders.

A short time later the Apache scout who led Dwyer's group of soldiers, slowly came into focus along the terrain. The awaiting ambushers knew that the soldiers' chances of following them was nil without their scout, so the best shooter between them selected the Apache. Each of the warriors were armed with a Winchester Rifle, which would allow them to shoot rapidly and reload.

With the soldiers following closely behind the scout, the Indians waited until they were within forty yards, before they opened fire. The first bullet discharged knocked the Apache off his horse and sent him tumbling backwards onto the ground. The other Cherokee warriors began shooting the soldiers off their horses, which created a hysteria among the cavalrymen. Lieutenant Dwyer and the rest of his troops returned fire at the five ambushers, while they rode about the base of the rocky slope. The ambushing Indians were hidden between the huge boulders along a hillside, and were difficult for the soldiers to get targets on. Both sides exchanged gunfire until Dwyer realized his soldiers' numbers were rapidly dwindling. To avoid losing all the soldiers under his command, the lieutenant sounded the retreat, following which they rode away and abandoned the chase.

General Bailey and his troops followed their Apache scout, until they reached the place where the Cherokee warriors they pursued, exited the river. The scout was unable to determine exactly how many warriors they were chasing until they reached that location, where he could clearly see the horse tracks and counted them. The general was none too pleased to hear, 'they had been chasing a possible decoy group,' while Chief Lakoatah and the others escaped in the other direction. Instead of continuing after the handful of decoys, General Bailey decided to rest their horses and waited until his lieutenant returned, with the rest of his troops. The soldiers had shown Chief Lakoatah and his war party what they were up against should they continued ravaging the homes of settlers. General Bailey thought his army persuaded the Indians to terminate their rampage, thus, his desire to continue chasing them decreased.

It wasn't until much later that evening, before Lieutenant Dwyer and thirty-nine of the soldiers placed under his command, slowly retuned to camp. When the Apache scout did not see his tracking comrade return, he needed no memo to inform him what had happened. As a result, Jackal walked to the edge of their camp, built a wooden fire, set it ablaze, then began mourning his colleague. Lieutenant Dwyer went directly to General Bailey's tent, where he disclosed everything that happened to his unit.

CHAPTER SEVEN

onathan Becket and six of his gun hands rode into the Town of Jasper, which was slowly regaining its vibrant atmosphere, with optimsm that the U.S Cavalry would terminate the Cherokee war party. They stopped in front the saloon and tied off their horses, before they continued into the bar. The instant they stepped through the revolving doors, the music, poker game, and chatter among the customers stopped, while everyone focused their attention on them. There were a few customers who frozen in their stance, as if a gang of robbers had entered, and ordered everyone 'to remain still!' The only people who reacted to the newcomers were those standing at the bar, who quickly cleared out the way as if Jonathan's entourage had prior reservations. The group of cattlemen and their boss walked to the bar counter, where the bartender simple sat up seven glasses, and slid Mr. Becket a bottle of Whiskey.

"What the hell is y'all staring at? Piano player, play some music, and everybody else get back to whatever y'all was doing," Quick Draw commanded!

All at once the music instantly began playing and the patrons started moving about, as if Quick Draw pressed the un-pause button on his remote. Becket and his helpers finished the entire bottle of Whiskey and got themselves mighty liquored up, to the extent that the boss began hallucinating. Jonathan began speculating that each of the saloon's clients were secretly discussing him, and thought he was responsible for the entire Indian uprising. The boss also thought they were conspiring vindictive things against him, even though everyone was simply enjoying themselves. The businessman staggered to the middle of the saloon, where he withdrew his firearm from the holster, and fired a shot in the ceiling. Three old men sitting at the table closest to the entrance immediately got up and exited the establishment, while others frightfully reacted to the thunderous scare.

"Them damn Indians have robbed you of your livelihoods… now look at y'all! Celebrating as if all was forgiven when they done killed a bunch of innocent white settlers. Joe Nedby burnt out, whole family killed, Tom Watson killed with his whole family, and even Old Man Parker out there by himself, are you just gonna accept that? I can hear your thoughts and you wanting to conspire against me! But at the end of it all, don't nothing belong to no damn Indian, not the land they live on, nor the food they eat! I don't care if they colored Indians or red skinned, if you ask me, they still need to be taught a lesson, for riding across this country of ours and doing good folks injustice," Mr. Becket argued!

"That's right Mr. Becket, if we don't teach them savages a lesson the next time the Sioux or the Apache gonna believe they can try the same shit," agreed Leonard Daws, who was seated around the Poker table!

"I done read in the papers, that they ain't caught that Chief Lakoatah and a bunch of them damn criminals, so we might just be doing the army a favor, killing off the rest a them bastards," Denis Mayers declared!

"We need to pay that Cherokee village a visit, and show them bastards why they must never conspire against us white folks! Now who's with me," Mr. Becket insinuated?

"Let's saddle up and ride," shouted a cowboy in agreement!

"Won't we need some sort of a plan or directions to their village," reasoned Frank Kerrigan?

"All we need is these rifles and pistols," answered Mr. Becket's gun hand Bobby!

"Wait Bobby he's right, we gotta get someone to show us the trail! And I think we know where we can find an Indian for the job," Mr. Becket stated!

"Yeah, let's go get them damn Indians," added another cowboy!

Each of the customers inside the saloon were under the influence of alcohol, therefore, they were all easily coerced into seeking revenge. As a result, instead of denouncing Jonathan's comments as racist, they sided with the bigot, and encouraged his prejudice. Deputy Eli Marks was making his way toward the saloon from the jailhouse, with his Double Barrel Buckshot Rifle over his shoulder, when he came across the three old men who fled from the establishment. Eli expected to find one or more drunk and disorderly customer who took his celebration a bit too far, at which he would arrest the culprit for public drunkenness, and have them spend the night in a jail cell.

"That you Earl, James, and Karl? Is you gentlemen coming from down by the saloon," Deputy Marks asked?

"We don't know nothing, deputy," James answered!

"You didn't hear it from us, but Mr. Becket's going off down there in his saloon," Earl exclaimed.

"Guess I can't arrest a man inside his own tavern, when he can just go sleep it off upstairs," Deputy Marks lamented.

"You have a good night deputy," Earl stated, as they passed each other and went about their business!

"Night gentlemen," Deputy Marks said!

Thirty-eight cowboys formed a vigilante mob and marched out to their horses, where they climbed into their saddles, and galloped to the far end of town. There was a handful of impoverished native Indians who lived in teepees on the edge of Jasper. The Indians were exiles from the Sioux and Cherokee villages, sent away for breaking the tribe's laws. Becket led his gang of drunken misfits to the Indians' camping ground and instructed two of his gun hands 'to find a Cherokee who would guide them!' Ralph and Bobby withdrew their Colt-45-barrel handguns, dismounted their horses, and entered two separate teepees, where the voices of children and females were heard screaming. Ralph exited his teepee emptyhanded and was about to enter a second tent, when Bobby dragged the male Indian known as Buffalo Tony from his domain. Buffalo Tony kicked and struggled to be released while being pulled by his left leg, until he found himself among the band of revenge seekers. Mr. Becket withdrew his Colt hand pistol and yanked back the hammer, which immediately caught the attention of the tussling Indian.

"Settle down boy, or I'll put a bullet in you right now," Mr. Becket threatened, at which Tony stopped struggling!

"What do you want," Tony asked?

"You are going to lead us to the Cherokee village or you and your whole family dies," Mr. Becket warned, hence, the Indian shook his head in agreement!

Deputy Eli reached the saloon seconds after the mob rode away, and curiously entered the establishment to determine where the group was heading, at such a late hour. The first person the deputy encountered was a female waitress named Monique, who was quite incensed about loosing the tips she had worked for. Crowder the barkeep had ran off with the mob, and left the saloon unattended, thus, Monique was in the middle of fixing herself a drink.

"Make mine a double Monique," requested Deputy Marks?

The waitress fixed both drinks and slid the deputy his glass.

"After all that servicing, those no-good bastards jumped up and ran outta here after listening to the boss for two minutes! You have any idea how long its been since we had strangers passed through town with money," Monique quarrelled?

Deputy Marks drank down the glass of Whiskey in one shot and asked, "where is all them fellows riding to at them hour?"

"Becket and his boys came up in here and talked up those liquored up fools into believing they aught to ride out to that Cherokee village and teach the rest a them damn Indians a lesson," Monique explained!

Deputy Marks picked up his Buckshot Rifle, threw it over his shoulder, got up from the barstool, and walked toward the entrance. As he approached the door the waitress who fixed herself a second drink shouted, "so ain't you gonna ride out there and stop those murdering bastards?"

"Nope, that's out of my jurisdiction," Deputy Marks stated, as he pushed through the revolving gates!

The mob of cowboys led by Mr. Becket aboard Tornado, reached the Cherokee village during the wee hour of the night, while the Indians rested comfortably. Shushuni was one of the few Indians awake, breast feeding her biological son Nicco, when she heard the outburst of gunfire. With the cowboys yelling while they shot Indians and set fire to their residents, there was no need for the young mother to curiously investigate. To save her children and herself, Shushuni grabbed Coyote and created a double pouch holder from a piece of cloth, in which she wrapped both boys. She then packed a few essentials in another cloth and wrapped them, then used her knife to cut a hole through the back of her teepee. Once outside Shushuni quickly ran deep into the woods and hid, where she could get a proper view of what was transpiring without compromising their safety.

When the angry mob arrived at their destination they stopped just beyond the village and made their final preparations. Quick Draw mercilessly stabbed their guide Buffalo Tony in the ribcage, then wiped his knife clean before he placed it in his shield. There was no need for handkerchiefs or cloaks to disguise their faces, considering they had no plans of leaving any survivors. Most of the cowboys lit torches, and ensured their weapons were loaded, before they made the final charge.

The gang of mercenaries rode into the village carrying their pistols and burning torches, which they threw onto the Indians' tents and burnt them to the ground. Mr. Becket and his followers shot and killed anyone who ran from their homes in protest, as they rode throughout the village and annihilated every Cherokee they spotted. Shushuni watched with tears flowing from her eyes and a heavy heart, as the cowboys destroyed her home and killed many of her family and friends.

Several of the Indians killed some of the cowboys, although there was a huge disparity with the ratio. Shushuni watched as some of the braves fought to defend their villagers, and thus allowed others to escape the horror. In many cases the white cowboys shot and killed women and children, who were trying to flee the massacre. Coyote continued comfortably sleeping during the shootings, but Nicco began fussing and refused to settle down. Fearing the cowboys might hear him, Shushuni removed him from the pouch and began breast feeding him. When other villagers who escaped began gathering around her, the young mother developed more confidence knowing she would not be the lone survivor.

CHAPTER
EIGHT

C hief Lakoatah's warriors who led General Bailey and most of his soldiers downriver, survived out in the wilderness for three days, before they returned to their village. Their people had rebuilt several tents and had a much smaller community, but they were ecstatic to have some of their warriors' home. The young braves felt responsible for the destruction brought on by the town's drunken cowboys, but mostly wished they had returned days earlier, to help defend their friends and families. Everybody wanted to know about the chief and their other warriors, however, the young braves' report of Lakoatah being wounded, created more despair than jubilation.

Chief Lakoatah and his warriors escaped into the mountains instead of returning to their reservation. Along the journey the chief drew increasingly weak and fell from his horse, thus, his companions chased away their horses and found a cave in which to hide. To confuse any tracker that might have been pursuing them, the warriors chopped branches with leaves from trees, then used them to sweep away their horse tracks. Walking Turtle was one of the survivors who had a vast knowledge of plants and herbs, therefore, he fetched four different types of leaves, prepared tea, and made an ointment to heal their leaders. The bullet was still lodged inside the chief's shoulder and had to be removed, so Walking Turtle gave him a piece of stick to bite onto, heated his knife in the fire, made an incision, and inserted his fingers to find the bullet. The procedure was extremely painful, but after a few minutes of poking around the young warrior found the bullet and extracted it, before he dressed the wound with the ointment, he grinded together.

The Cherokee Chief had lost a lot of blood and was incredibly weak, so he fell unconscious during the procedure and slept for the next seventy-eight hours. While the chief rested, his warriors remained by his side and only left the cave to fetch food, water, firewood, and herbs. They arranged lookout teams of two people throughout the day, to ensured they did not encounter any mishaps with guards falling asleep on duty. The Indians were in a remote area where it was impossible to get any news on what was developing across the country. Due to their predicament, they knew nothing of the destruction of their village or what President Jackson was forced to do as a result. When news of the slaughter that occurred on the Cherokee reservation reached the President, he had to stop the annihilation of an American tribe of native people. To do this, President Jackson wrote an injunction declaring Chief Lakoatah and the rest of his warriors, exempt from all legal charges.

Most of the warrior had low moral following the deaths of their close friends and siblings, during the cavalry encounter. The days which followed only presented added emotional strain with the injury to their leader, whose recovery was at first uncertain. When Lakoatah finally opened his eyes and called out, those who were with him inside the cave jumped for joy like little children, then gathered around him. There were only seven remaining African American Indian males among the group, and unlike their native brothers they were the rarest of breeds. Even though the chief was not back to his normal self, having him conscious steadily built the warriors' confidence, knowing they would have his guidance.

Chief Lakoatah sustained the devastating loss of his eldest son during the train conflict and was rather angry he lost his successor. To commemorate those killed, later that night the Indians relieved both guards of their duty for several hours and held a private vigil. Lakoatah sat at the helm of his warriors with the assistance of his personal physician, who saved his life with all the different treatments he administered. The chief first recognized and thanked Walking Turtle for nursing him back to health, as he positively would have died without the healing remedies. All the remaining warriors were brought to sit beside their campfire and held hands, to define their strength and unity, while Chief Lakoatah prayed to their forefathers and anointed those killed into the Spirit Realm.

The Cherokee warriors remained hidden for another week with the belief they were still being hunted by the U.S cavalry. The Indians were aware that the soldiers had visited their village, so they contemplated what they needed to do to keep their villagers safe. By the end of the week, the chief had gotten strong enough to travel the long-distance home, if he need to ruggedly maneuver a horse. The group of Indians resourcefully walked and made their way across treacherous terrain, without being spotted. They travelled mostly throughout the nights, hunkered down during the hot days, before they reached their reservation after nearly a month hiatus. From the instant they stepped on the outskirts of their land, all the Indians knew there was something wrong long before they reached the village. None of them knew their village had been reduced to an empty field, filled with patches of burnt rubble. At the sight of their destroyed homes, several of the warriors crumbled to their knees in sorrow, with the belief that all had been lost.

After a few minutes of heart wrenching pain, the warriors heard several alert whistles from the bushes. Chief Lakoatah's mate Shiloh cautiously emerged from the bushes thereafter, followed by the other survivors who lived through the cowboys' malicious attack. Even the warriors who had to separate to trick the cavalrymen, were elated to see their colleagues had returned safely. Everyone began shouting a triumphant scream, after the villagers had assumed the worst. Shiloh had lacerations across her face, a broken arm in a sling, and walked with a noticeable limp, after being beaten within fractions of her life. Evidence of the tortures experienced by the villagers was also visible on some of the children, who had welts, red pigmentations from cowboy's boot heels to their anatomies, and fractured limbs. Many of the returned warriors called out to their wives and children, who had been murdered and burnt inside their tents. There were only sixteen children saved, the eldest of which was Chief Lakoatah's youngest son Chivalro, who was nine years of age.

Walking Turtle had leapt into the ashes, of what once used to be the home he shared with his woman and daughter, wherein he rolled around in the filth weeping. The other survivors had transferred the remains of the deceased to their graveyard, where they granted them a proper resting place. Shiloh and the others had relocated the village three-hundred yards from the original location for safety concerns, but the members of the war party thought they were eradicated. Neither Lakoatah's party nor any of the other survivors knew of their acquittal by President Jackson, therefore, by the next morning the chief again relocated their entire village.

Chief Lakoatah brought his people fifteen kilometres west of their temporary home, to another location on their reservation, where they secretly rebuilt their village. Shushuni had helped to console Walking Turtle during his depressive state, after he learnt about his murdered family. Because of their familiarity with each other, it was not surprising they became inseparable thereafter, and constructed a teepee together. Walking Turtle was such great friends with both Nicco and Coyote's fathers, that Shushuni made an excellent choice when she chose him as her next partner.

The Cherokee female trusted he would grow the boys in their fathers' likeness and advised them of whom their biological fathers were. Within a month of their coupling Shushuni became pregnant, which was the most pleasant news the tribe had received since their relocation. Following weeks of mourning the losses of their loved ones, the Indians held a joyful celebration where they bestowed blessing unto the new parents. The Nevada Indians' entire focus had changed, to where their primary directive became the enlargement of their population, which was a mere fraction of what they were.

The Cherokee Chief knew the importance of a larger Indian community, instead of their reduced numbers, so he had to inspire his villagers to build relationships and thus reproduced. There were five young ladies expecting their first children, whose mates were killed during the raids. Many of the females had lost their husbands in the raids, and many of the warriors returned to find their mates killed by the cowboys. Despite the widespread sorrows, Chief Lakoatah began holding challenge events, where both males and females participated in friendly games, to compete for each other's affections.

The competition offered a few women who had previously been overlooked by men in the village, the opportunity to find a husband. Two of such females were the Cherokee Chief's daughters, whose body types were those of larger sized women. The Cherokee Indian males participated in bow and arrow shooting challenges, wrestling challenges, and spear throwing challenges, to determine who would win the female prizes. Prior to the men's challenges, the females participated in tug-a-war matches, where they demonstrated their strength and skills. The rope used was weaved from a slain Buffalo's skin, which was stretched while it dried in the hot sun, before the Indians created the long and durable product. With the contestants ready to compete, the Indians drew a line across which competitors should not cross, or their opponents would be deemed the winner. While each event was held in good humor, the objective was to illustrate to the men the sorts of wives they would be competing for.

Following the ladies' challenge events, the community enjoyed a festive evening, where they roasted a deer, and prepared a huge meal for the entire village. After they ate their fill, the warriors sat around a huge bonfire and played their musical instruments, while their champions from the day's events danced around in a circle, to further entice their interested counterparts. There were no interactions permitted between either sex before the challenges, unless the male and female made their decision to join known to the chief.

When the men competed the following day, each of them surpassed their physical capabilities to acquire the more desirable females. The unwed warriors tried their best to even win the affections of the pregnant widows, before their choices dwindled to Chief Lakoatah's daughters. The warriors respected and followed the Cherokee Chief into battle, but none of them wanted to win the affections of his overweight daughters. Neither of his daughters were ever married, were renowned as the gossipers of their village, and were both well beyond forty years of age.

Chief Lakoatah and his wife could not wait to see who would finally remove their daughters from their cramped teepee, therefore, they awaited the men's competitions with great anticipation. The rules for each match specified that 'the warrior stepped forth and stated the female for whom they competed,' therefore, each winner got awarded their prize. Throughout the day, Lakoatah and Shiloh watched as the warriors won and selected the more elegant females, until the competitors had dwindled to two. The only females left were the ones considered less desirable and neither of the warriors were ecstatic about their choices. The final four trophies included their daughters, another large sized female, and a slightly handicapped squaw, who was conceived with a deformed left hand.

The final two competitors faced off in a bow and arrow accuracy challenge, where the closest arrow to the center circle was deemed the winner. The first challenger stepped to the line, aimed at the score board, and completely missed the target. After the warrior's arrow sailed pass the target, the second challenger stepped to the line, and fired his arrow into the ground a foot before the target. Following the second participant's shot, the first warrior again stepped to the line and fired his arrow even further than before. Some of the spectators began chuckling at the two challengers, when the second shooter stepped to the line, and fired his arrow next to his last. It became obvious that both excellent archers were intentionally missing the score board, so Chief Lakoatah shouted, "we shall measure each of your next arrows, for the winner!"

The first shooter step to the line and fired his arrow five inches from the center of the target. With the suspense at an unnerving rate, the second shooter stepped to the line, took aim, and fired his arrow directly in the center. Before the chief could enquire about the warrior's choice, the Indian spun around and called out the handicapped female's name, which shocked Shiloh and her husband. The last warrior's eyes met with Lakoatah's, who gave him a stern look. The depressed warrior slowly hung his head and selected their youngest daughter, which was a relief for the chief to hear.

CHAPTER
NINE

Geneeral Bailey and his troops stopped at a route crossing, where their Apache scout Jackal, spoke with the cavalry leader. Jackal was mounted on his horse and held the reigns to his deceased colleague's horse, which had Sasha's dead body aboard.

"I thank you General, for allowing me to bring Sasha back to his family," Jackal stated!

"Just make sure you find me a damn good replacement tracker like Sasha, then ride back to the fort! This little business shouldn't take us too long," General Bailey ordered!

"Yes Sir, General Bailey," Jackal declared, before he selected a different route from his unit!

The cavalry then continued to the Cherokee village on official state business. When General Bailey and his army rode into the former Cherokee village, the army veteran was stunned to see all the destroyed teepees. The general went back to the village to issue the president's declaration, but he had no idea the xenophobic cowboys had previously visited to exterminate the Indians. There were no deceased bodies scattered about the village, which led the general to believe there were survivors, who buried the dead.

Lieutenant Dwyer sent several soldiers to check the surrounding for survivors or signs that indicated where they went. Without their trusted scout to find a consistent pattern illustrating where the Cherokee Indians may had gone, the soldiers had no choice but to turn around and leave. There was multiple evidence left throughout the village that proved the Indians were attacked by cowboys, so the general made note of what he saw, to file his report back to the president.

Before returning to the fort, the general travelled to the Town of Jasper, where he left the vast numbers of soldiers outside of town, then rode in to visit with the local sheriff. While riding through town, General Bailey and his escorts rode by Becket's Saloon, where the cattleman and his gun hands were lounging on the sidewalk. Mister Becket tipped his hat to the general, who looked at him and acknowledged his pleasantries, by slightly bowing his head.

"Ain't nobody in this town gonna help you army folks general," Quick Draw shouted!

The general proceeded to Sheriff Hopkins' jailhouse, where he and his three escorts descended their hoses, and walked up the stairs to the structure. Sheriff Hopkins was seated behind his desk, with his deputy across the room, cleaning his Double Barrel Buckshot Rifle. General Bailey's guards waited outside the door, while he entered to address the sheriff. While it was against the law for any Indian tribe to attack and kill white folks, it was also a criminal offense to kill Indians, therefore, the general had to uphold the law.

"Howdy General, what brings you back into town," Sheriff Hopkins stated?

"Sheriff Hopkins there was an incident out on the Cherokee reservation. You wouldn't happen to know anything about that now, would you," General Bailey asked?

"May I offer you some coffee General," Sheriff Hopkins asked?

"I sure wouldn't mind a cup, it's starting to get a bit nippy out there," General Bailey answered!

The sheriff got up and walked over to the coffee kettle and poured the general a cup. "What sort a incident you referring to General?"

"It seemed like some cowboys visited them unarmed Indians and burnt their village to the ground," General Bailey stated!

"Sorry to hear that General, but their reservation is outta my jurisdiction," Sheriff Hopkins declared!

"Sheriff Bailey it is a federal offense to attack native Indians, regardless of what town folks may think," began the general!

"General, a few weeks backs I went out one night to do my security walk round town. When I reached Becket Saloon a group of men rode off heading outta town. I went inside and asked one the waitress where they was heading at that late hour, and she said they was fitting to ride out to the reservation," Deputy Marks said!

"Why the hell didn't you tell me all this before Eli," Sheriff Hopkins asked?

"Sorry sheriff, but by time I got back that night you was already gone home, then by morning I guess, I must have forgot to mention it," Deputy Marks responded!

"Who was some of the men in that late night posse," General Bailey asked?

"Mister Becket, his help, and a bunch a drunken town folks," Deputy Marks said!

"I thank you for your help gentlemen," General Bailey stated, before he finished the coffee, got up, and left!

*

Jackal removed his U.S army uniform along the trail and hid the clothes inside his saddlebag, before he reached his Apache village. The scout rode into the village, where a crowd of residents began gathering, and walked behind his partner's horse to their destination. When Jackal reached the teepee, which belonged to his deceased partner's family, he stopped and called out to the parents. A mid-aged female exited the dwelling with two grown men and a younger female. The woman was Sasha's mother, and the four others his brothers and his sister. As soon as the woman saw the horse with her son's body, she and her daughter broke down and began crying, while the brothers stepped forth and helped to take the body off the horse. The Apache scout stepped to his partner's mother and handed her a wrapped parcel, that was given to him by General Bailey. The parcel contained a flag of the United States of America, a letter that thanked the parents for their son's service, and $50 for burial.

With the body already properly wrapped, the Indians began chanting burial hymns, as they went directly to their burial ground to anoint the body to their ancestors. Most of the Apache Indians did not care for the white man's army, so many of them shunned Jackal for working with them. Despite the mixed emotions, the deceased scout's family members were considered wealthy, due to the aide he had provided them. Sasha's three brothers were involved in the burial process, but as soon as they were free of their obligations, they spoke with Jackal to determine how their sibling died.

Jackal made sure he informed the brothers and their friends, that Sasha was killed by the Cherokee during an ambush. The Apache considered the Cherokee their rivals, so many of the youngsters wanted revenge immediately. When the Apache Chief heard the mob developing, he quelled their excitement by reminding them 'that the scouts were officially on white man's business!' As a result, none of the warriors were permitted to retaliate in aide of the Caucasians.

Jackal visited his parents and spent some time with them before he left for the fort. The scout brought tobacco, whiskey, and money for his father, who lived a good life with their son being employed. The army gave their scouts a few days of vacation time each year, which was usually the time they visited the village. While partaking of a drink with his father inside their teepee, his deceased partner's brother went by to reason with him.

"Jackal! Jackal, it is Shamar," yelled the visitor!

The scout emerged from within, at which both men shook hands, then walked over toward the horses.

"My family thanks you for brining my brother home," Shamar said!

"Your brother was a great tracker in the white man's army, it was my honor to bring him to rest on the grounds of his forefathers," Jackal stated!

"My brother has done great things for his family, regardless of what many around here think about the white man's army! I too wish to help my family, and become great tracker like my brother," Shamar said!

Jackal placed his hand on the warrior's shoulder and answered, "this is good decision for you and your family! The army needs Apache trackers, the best! Go get your things, we leave---!"

"I have my horse, my rifle! I need not return, I am ready to leave this place," Shamar declared!

Jackal walked into his parents' teepee, where he said his goodbyes, then collected his saddlebag and rifle, before he exited. Shamar was already aboard his horse holding the reigns to Jackal's horse. The Apache scout placed his saddlebag on his horse and leapt aboard, following which both men rode out of the village.

CHAPTER
TEN

Despite all his wealth Jonathan Becket's craving for more power was far from quenched, therefore, he entered into the next political election to become the mayor of Jasper. The incumbent Mayor Victor Rolley had been in office for a decade and was very much respected by the residents in town, so defeating him would not be an easy task. Jonathan also had a number of business incentives to becoming mayor, top of the list was getting rid of the town's troublesome sheriff, with whom he was constantly in heated arguments. Jasper was a small town with a population well under eight hundred people, yet was a major hub for prospectors and settlers seeking supplies. There were at least two stagecoaches that passed through town daily and transported passengers to other states across the country.

While shipping his customers' livestock to different states across the country, Mr. Becket passed through several big towns where he borrowed ideas for businesses. One such enterprise involved whores and topless women performing, and catering to the needs of the saloon's customers, which the lawful church attending folks of Jasper rightfully declined. Even though several of the other businessmen throughout Jasper were intrigued with allowing such an establishment, Mayor Rolley who was a devoted Christian, declined the petition. According to the Mayor's ruling, 'indulging in such lewd behavior would change their town for the worst, and would not be of benefit to their citizens in the long term!' Jonathan knew that once he became mayor he would have the power to do whatever he wanted, therefore, he did everything necessary to defeat Mayor Rolley.

Mr. Becket began bringing his family to church, being polite and courteous to the citizens on the street, and a host of other kind-hearted gestures he never previous practiced. Regardless of what he did, half of the good citizens of Jasper hated him for not only starting the Indian uprising, but also nearly exterminating the Nevada Cherokee tribe. Word of Indian Tony's abduction and suspected murder had also circulated throughout the town, but nobody dared to publicize anything of the incident, with fears of what could happen. While on the surface Jonathan pretended as if he was a changed man who wanted better for Jasper, behind the scenes his Gun-hands intimidated voters with threats and physical violence.

*

Three months prior to the election Beth Becket and her son Horace travelled to San Diego, California, to purchase clothing fabrics and other supplies for her store. Beth had made a few such trips throughout the years, wherein she often left for up to a week, therefore, Jonathan had grown accustomed to her business practices. Following the conclusion of her transactions, Beth was forced to spend an additional night and thus extended their stay at the local motel.

The next stagecoach that travelled to Jasper was scheduled to leave at 6:00 AM, and Beth had no intentions of missing it, so she brought Horace to a local tavern to eat an early supper, before they turned in for the evening. There were no other customers inside the tavern except for the lady who served Horace and Beth, hence, she returned behind the counter cleaning drinking glasses with a cloth. While they ate, a loud ruckus erupted upstairs, slightly before a cowboy wearing his socks, hat, Long-John Underwear, and had the remains of his belongings underneath his arm, came backpedalling down the stairs. Horace could not help but to look up at the incident, where he saw a female holding a Remington 36mm hand pistol to the man's groin.

"Horace Becket, you turn back around this instant and eat your food," Beth threatened, at which her son did as he was told!

"The next time before you get all drunk and lose your money gambling, instead of spending it on me, think about this Tiny Tim," threatened the whore as she yanked back the pistol's hammer!

"No, no, no please don't Betty Lee… I swear it'll never happen again," pled Tiny Tim!

"You best get your ass home to your wife, before I send you over to Doctor Culliver instead," Betty Lee instructed!

"Ri-ri-right away Betty Lee," nervously responded the man!

The man turned around once he got released by Betty Lee, scurried down the remaining stairs, and ran from the establishment, while he stumbled to put

49

on his trousers. Horace chuckled at the sight of the grown man trying to get dressed in public, then stopped abruptly when Beth gave him an unpleasant stare. Betty Lee walked down to the bar where the waitress fixed her a shot of whiskey, the instant she sat down. The entire ordeal gave Beth an idea, therefore, she waved over Betty Lee and asked her to join them? Beth believed that the tough-minded female could help her husband capture the mayoral election back in Jasper, and thus offered her a contract worth ten-thousand-dollars plus incentives.

Betty Lee was an incredibly beautiful and sensuous twenty-five-year-old blond, who worked as a local whore in town. The opportunity to make the amount of money being proposed was the chance of a lifetime for the young beauty, hence, she graciously accepted, then listened to the details of the plot. Even though Betty Lee agreed to the terms, Beth was skeptical she would uphold her end of the bargain, once she thought through the dangers. To avoid being scammed or robbed, Beth only left enough money to cover the stagecoach ride, then guaranteed a portion of the payment once Betty Lee reached Jasper.

Early the next morning, Mrs. Becket and her son boarded the first stagecoach and left town. Horace was so tired after he was awakened that he quickly went back to sleep the moment the stagecoach departed. To avoid any speculations of deceitfulness, Betty Lee boarded her stagecoach the following day, to work in a part of the country she had never visited. There were not many single women relocating to small towns like Jasper, especially women of such beauty and grace like Betty Lee, therefore, news of her lengthy stay travelled quickly through the town.

It was well into the night when the stagecoach arrived in Jasper, and Betty Lee dismounted. Her first impression of the town was that "it appeared quite lifeless," still she looked forward to elevating the excitement. Upon arrival Betty Lee checked into a local motel, where the stagecoach driver brought her luggage up to her room. Ten minutes later while she freshened up from the long ride, a knock sounded at her door. Betty Lee responded and found a female holding a bag standing outside, so without any questions she allowed her entry. The woman's name was Eve, and she was an employee of Mrs. Becket, who sent her solely to drop off the bag.

"I was told to bring this to you ma'am," Eve said without mentioning anyone specifically!

Betty Lee took the bag and looked inside, then smiled to herself at the amount of money enclosed. With their business concluded, Eve threw her vale over her head, opened the door, looked both sides of the hallway, then took precaution as she made her way out of the establishment. After Eve left Betty Lee bolted the door behind her, threw all the currencies on the bed, then dived onto it, and rolled around like a child at the playground.

The next day Betty Lee visited Mayor Rolley's office to introduce herself and acquire some living arrangement advice. The long walk to the Mayor's office located near the town's main entrance was quite eventful, as the locals reacted as if they had never seen an elegantly dressed lady before. Every resident Betty Lee passed along the sidewalk was indeed polite, however, they had awful habits of staring and would watch her after she had gone by. Windows and shutters that were closed began popping open as nosey residents fought to get a peek of the day's biggest gossip.

A cowboy riding by on his horse got so entranced by Betty Lee's beauty, that he gazed way too long and steered his horse into a stationed wagon. Even Betty Lee was forced to giggle to herself, when the cowboy's horse stopped abruptly, and threw him from the saddle. The embarrassed cowboy got propelled from his horse and broke several bottles of illegal Moonshine, when he crashed into the back of the wagon. The scent of alcohol quickly became prominent, as the cowboy slowly sat forward and surveyed the damages. The two men to whom the wagon belonged came running from the saloon, at which one of them aimed their weapons at the cowboy responsible, who quickly threw both his hands high in the air. The Liquor Peddlers confiscated the cowboy's horse and doubled up on the saddle, before they galloped out of town.

Mayor Rolley's wife Amanda, who served as his personal secretary, granted Betty Lee permission to enter when she knocked. Amanda then asked Betty Lee to wait patiently, while she enquired if the mayor was available for unscheduled visit? Mrs. Rolley who exhibited no signs of jealousy when she spoke with Betty Lee, entered her husband's office, and could clearly be heard arguing over, "who and why the young beauty came by to visit?" After a few minutes, the secretary exited the room and asked Betty Lee to enter. Regardless of the tension, the blond beauty walked by Amanda and entered the Mayor's office, where she closed the door, introduced herself, and was offered a seat to sit to converse. Instead of returning to her workstation Amanda snuck close to the door and tried to eavesdrop on their conversation.

"Now, what can I do for you Miss," Mayor Rolley began?

"Betty Lee, Mister Mayor," the female responded!

"Such a lovely name for such a beautiful creature of God! How may I help you Miss Betty Lee," Mayor Rolley questioned?

"I've grown tired of living in the big cities mayor, and would like to settle into a small town like this, buy myself a house, and raise some chickens," Betty Lee answered.

"Well, a transaction like that takes money Miss Betty Lee; and I didn't see you ride into town with a husband," Mayor Rolley exclaimed.

"Oh, excuse me did I say miss, I meant former misses! See my husband recently died and after all those years in one place, I've decided that I need a fresh start," Betty Lee exclaimed.

"Since you put it that way, I'm sure we'll be able to find you proper lodging here in Jasper. I doubt you heard that we'll be having an election here in the next few months, it sure be helpful if I could get your vote," Mayor Rolley declared!

"I guess that all depends on what you can do for me, Mister Mayor," Betty Lee teased!

"You sure came to see the right man Miss Betty Lee," Mayor Rolley boasted!

Betty Lee was seated across the table from Mayor Rolley and had her right leg crossed over her left, therefore, she slowly untangled them, while ensuring she exposed her undergarment, before she repositioned her feet. Mayor Rolley's eyes widened, as his smile flashed across his face, which suggested to Betty Lee that he could be persuaded to commit adultery.

"How bout you help me settle in this here town, and I'd be happy to give you my vote," negotiated Betty Lee?

"You got yourself a deal Miss Betty Lee," agreed Mayor Rolley, at which they shook hands to honor the deal!

Within a week Betty Lee found a home with the assistance of Mayor Rolley and became a first-time homeowner. The house was a single bedroom occupancy and cost the new town's resident five hundred dollars, which was covered under her incentives deal clause. It was nearly impossible to keep secrets in such a small town, so Mrs. Rolley found out Victor had a major involvement in Betty Lee home purchase, so she forbade him to ever deal with her thereafter. To show her gratitude Betty Lee sent an invitation to the Mayor for a private dinner, but he declined to answer and gave no justification for his lack of response. The date for the mayoral election was getting closer, and Victor had a substantial lead over his opponent Jonathan Becket, who could not gain any traction or get individuals to switch their votes.

A month prior to the election, Eve and Quick Draw visited Betty Lee late one night, and brought her some white powdery substance, on a piece of paper, with instructions on how to use it. The gun hand's vicious reputation was well known throughout parts of the west, plus Betty Lee had seen him around town, and observed how people revered him. Betty Lee believed all the stories she had heard about Quick Draw, so when he threatened that 'he would kill and bury her somewhere in the desert if she did not provide what they wanted,' she trusted every word! By then it was nearly a month since Betty Lee last had any contact with the Mayor, hence, she grew incredibly scared of what would happen should she fail to accomplish what had been demanded of her.

Mayor Rolley heeded his wife's warning and avoided all interactions with Betty Lee, until five days before the election, when he became overconfident about his victory, and decided to celebrate prematurely. The Mayor went to Betty Lee's house after meeting with some supporters one night, expecting to partake of a few shots of Whiskey, then fondled with his host a bit. Betty Lee graciously welcomed in the mayor and flirted with him, before she went off to prepare their refreshments. While fixing the liquor, the conniving female threw some of the powdery substance into his drink. Betty Lee was so nervous she would get caught, that she sprinkled some of the powder onto the side of the glass, and was in the process of wiping it clean, when the Mayor walked over, and picked up his drink. Victor quickly emptied the glass and placed it on the table, then began massaging his host's shoulders, to sexually entice her. Betty Lee began walking back to her bed, during which the mayor began noticeably staggering.

Mayor Rolley was guided onto the bed, where he looked up at Betty Lee and saw multiplied images of the female. The mayor realized he had been drugged and pointed his finger at Betty Lee, seconds before he tumbled backwards onto the bed unconscious. When Mayor Rolley awakened, he was at home in his own bed, had a massive headache, yet felt relieved that his experience must have been a dream. After he crawled out of bed, Victor walked out into the days room where he realized he was alone. He called out to his wife several times and could not locate her anywhere, until he saw a written note on the table. As soon as he scanned over the first few words, Victor fell back onto a chair, as tears began rolling from his eyes. Two days following that incident a photograph of Betty Lee mounted on top of a naked Mayor Rolley appeared in the town's newspaper. The scandal cost Mayor Rolley the election, as voters turned to the only other option and cast their votes for Jonathan Becket, who became the new mayor of Jasper.

CHAPTER
ELEVEN

With all their couples assorted, the Cherokee community prepared for their first ever mass wedding. Some of the participants were not fully healed after they had lost their significant others, but for the survival of their tribe, it was imperative that they procreated and increased their numbers. Chief Lakoatah was not thrilled about what they had to do, however, with less than a half of their population remaining, the Nevada Cherokee Tribe was on the cusp of extinction. The Chief among everyone else had the most conflictive sentiments regarding marrying most of the couples, considering he was the person who performed their first marriage ceremony.

The day of the weddings was both joyful and sad for the community, which had to release the past and accept the future, for the survival of their people. It was indeed a tough time for the entire tribe, therefore, most of the villagers wept throughout or sometime during that day. The Cherokee people prepared their largest fest in years, which had food and drinks in abundance. With such a huge and festive event, everyone throughout the community were obligated to attend, thus, there were no lookouts posted to warn the Indians of intruders. Chief Lakoatah never met with General Bailey to discuss their status, but the Cherokee Chief had received a summery of the president's ruling, so they had no cause for concern.

*

Shamar's youngest brother Calian, was one of the warriors who wanted the mob of angry Apache to attack the Cherokee people, for revenge over the killing of their army scout sibling. Money was not considered a major commodity among the Indians, who mainly survived by hunting, fishing, and the vegetation they grew. Even though the Apache lived simple lives, the ability to acquire goods with money, placed some of their villagers in unique categories. Calian's employed sibling gave his family the ability to live comfortable lives, therefore, most of his relatives were considered influential to some of the villagers. As a young child growing in the village, Calian had things which no other youth his age could afford. During his brother's visits over the years, Calian introduced his friends to many sample items from the Caucasian world. Because of his controversial family, many of the youths who grew with Calian followed him, as if he were their leader.

Calian was an extremely stubborn twenty-one-year-old, who felt privileged because of the things he was provided as a child. While most of his friends had to wait for hand-me-downs, or some family member to pass away, before they got their first Winchester Rifle, Calian was given a brand-new firearm for his seventh birthday. The young rambunctious Apache never wavered from his arrogance and became more vindictive with the slaying of his favorite brother. Instead of heeding the warning of their superior, who refused to go to war over an issue that the white man started, Calian's chose to disobey orders and avenged his sibling.

Calian and his close friends left the village most evenings and strolled down to the river, where they smoked pre-rolled tobacco and drank liquor. The young warriors would often discuss the beautiful young females in the village or joked about the latest gossip. After getting his five best friends intoxicated a few nights after Shamar departed for the army, Calian dared the bunch of thrill seekers to accompany him to the Cherokee reservation. Both Indian villages were almost six hours apart from each other, so the warriors knew they were in for a long ride.

One of the warriors had recently lost his horse, so they first needed to borrow one for the journey. The six young troublemakers waited until later that night, after most of the warriors had fallen asleep, before they snuck back into the village, entered the horse pen, and removed a horse. To deject the animal from making noises during the process, the Indians continuously fed the horse apples. After they walked the horse a short distance away, Calian and his comrades leapt aboard the bareback animals and rode off into the night.

It was well into the morning when the six Apache youths rode onto the Cherokee's reservation. They cautiously advanced until they came upon the abandoned village's border, where they dismounted off their horses, and snuck closer for a better view. After they maneuvered through some bushes, the Indians walked out onto the clearing where the Cherokees used to reside. Tracking and deciphering clues were traits the Apache passed on from generation to generation, so the troublemakers began looking around the camp for evidence of what happened. After a few minutes of searching, one of the Indians called out to his friends, and indicated that 'he found the survivors' tracks!'

The troublesome youths travelled from their reservation in Death Valley, California, to unknown lands they had never visited. They rode slowly through the bushes following the tracks left behind, until they reached the place where the Cherokee relocated. The Apache young men hid their horses and crawled to a survey point, from which they watched the villagers hustled about. The troublemakers knew nothing of the Cherokee's way of living, but it was obvious they were preparing for some festive event.

Out of curiosity the group of Indians decided to wait around and watched whatever type of function the Cherokee villagers were having. Most of Calian's friends were exhausted after they rode throughout the night, so they returned to their horses and went to sleep. Calian chose to keep watch and ensured his friends were not found while they rested, which could have been detrimental for them all. By midday Calian was also nodding as his fell asleep, before the Cherokee villagers started beating their drums and shaking their rattles, as the festivities got on the way. The Apache troublemaker slowly snuck away from his watchpoint and went to alert his associates.

By the time the band of misfits returned, the entire Cherokee community had gotten involved in the proceedings. The local Indians were parading their engaged couples around the village, as they began the long wedding ceremony. All the wedding participants wore colorful beads and feathers, which was customary for those being wed. None of the Apache watchers had ever witnessed a Cherokee wedding, therefore, they were intrigued by the multiple couples. After the local men paraded the celebrating husbands around the village, the women paraded their soon to be wives thereafter. The husbands were then brought before Chief Lakoatah after the parade, at which the chief instructed them 'to form a line to his left!' Once the ladies finished parading the wives around the village, they were aligned across from their husbands, to the chief's right.

The chief gave a lengthy speech which bored the Apache spectators, who could not hear a word of what he was saying. Following the speech, Chief Lakoatah called each couple to be wed, then used a piece of string and tied their left and right hands together, while he blessed their marriage. Many of the females getting married cried throughout the ceremony, having lost their beloved spouses, yet were forced to remarry.

Even though the young Apache Indians agreed to follow Calian, none of them knew the deviance within his heart. While his companions thought only of boasting to their peers about their brave exploit, Calian was determined to get his revenge. Once the Cherokee villagers began partaking of their huge feast, the troublemakers' stomachs began growling, having not eaten anything that day. There were only a few hours of daylight left, so considering the long distance they still had to travel, Calian suggested 'they retrieved their horses to take their leave!'

The six misfits went back to the place where they tied their horses and retrieved them. Calian demanded they took one final closer look at the festivities, before they began the long journey home. Instead of returning to their surveillance location on the hill, Calian took a different route that brought his entourage much closer to the village. When the young Apache warriors crept to the treeline on the edge of the village, they remained in the shadows and watched, while the celebrators enjoyed the ambiance. All the Cherokee villagers were unaware they were under surveillance, until Calian unexpectedly took aim with his rifle, and shot one of the braves who was walking across the compound.

The revenge seeker began yelling their traditional Apache war cry, before he spun his horse in the opposite direction and rode away. Several of the Cherokee warriors began shooting into the woods, which forced Calian's friends to hastily take their leave. By the time some of the Cherokee fighters mounted their horses and rode after the troublemakers, it was too late to catch any of them, with the separation they had created. The Apache young men did not look back and rode hard until they were on their own reservation, in Death Valley. The Cherokee pursuers caught definitive images of the attackers which proved they were Apache scouts, before they returned to the camp.

Calian shot the Cherokee Indian in the upper chest region and thought he killed the warrior. However, once the pursuit Indians returned, they found the man being treated by the female healer. The bullet struck the warrior in the right shoulder and was still lodged inside, yet pitched him to the ground with force. Had the injured warrior been killed, their festive day would have transformed to one of sorrow, which would have been too much for some to bare. The warriors who rode after the Apache troublemakers spoke with Chief Lakoatah, who was confused by the entire event.

"They were Apache, Chief Lakoatah," one of the pursuers stated!

"Why the Apache choose to attack us now," Chief Lakoatah argued?

Most of the villagers looked around curiously at each other, before a member of the war party recalled the shootout they had versus a group of soldiers.

"We did kill one Apache, Chief Lakoatah! Scout for the army, who was leading the soldiers after us," one of the colored warriors stated!

"Now the Apache knows our numbers, the white man may also know our numbers! My people hear me!... Until we are much stronger in numbers, we are weaker than a pact of wolves! For this reason alone, we must become stronger in numbers, or we risk getting extinguished!"

Despite the festive change because of the shooting, the chief's observation led many of the newly married females to take their mate's hands into theirs. Other couples began embracing, as they accepted their responsibilities to procreate and increase their tribe. The attempted assassination helped to unite the community, which had suffered tremendously since the raids. Chief Lakoatah was concerned for his villagers, who were accessible to any forms of attacks at that junction. They had relocated twice over the past few months, neverthe-less, the chief seriously contemplated moving their village again.

CHAPTER
TWELVE

The town of Jasper, which was renowned for being a peaceful and law-abiding place, changed once Jonathan Becket became the mayor. Most of the town's citizens lived simple lives and preferred living in rural type areas, instead of the larger and busier city dwellers. Mayor Becket wanted the town to become a major city, yet like every developed nation with a growing population, their biggest issue became jobs. The previous mayor fought to maintain the culture of the town, and thus refrained from issuing certain types of Business Permits, which in turn reduced the types of visitors in town, and the number of available employments.

As an intellectual businessman who also had his personal agenda, Jonathan began issuing Business Permits to developers who wanted to establish all sorts of businesses in Jasper. To attract new residents and interest in their town, one of the strategies implemented was a rumor, that began one day when Jonathan noticed an old prospector searching for gold in the nearby river. Mister Becket thought of an idea and approached the prospector with a business proposition. When the old man who was getting up in age and wished to retire, agreed to Becket's proposition, they devised a plan to start the rumor at his Hardware Store. The fib that was eventually posted in the newspaper, was of the gold prospector who was rumored to have found gold nuggets in the river, just outside of Jasper.

The store clerk from the hardware store added to the dishonesty when he told folks, 'he weighed and exchanged the prospector's gold for supplies!' Mister Becket's banker also corroborated the lie, when he disclosed that 'he processed the nuggets, following which he deposited the proceeds into Mayor

Becket's business account!' Because of this prospector's dishonesty, people began flocking to Jasper from across the country. For decades, the Christian folks in town had denounced prostitution and Whore Houses, but within a month of Jonathan taking office, the first pay for sex establishment went under construction.

When the building began getting erected and the citizens found out what type of business was being opened, a huge backlash erupted where concerned citizens held a Town Hall meeting, to discuss stopping the project. At the Town Hall event, in order to maintain peace inside the hall, Deputy Eli Marks collected every man's pistol at the entrance, then searched them to ensure they had no other weapons hidden. Mayor Becket was not invited, yet, showed up at the meeting with six of his gun-hands and his wife. The mayor sat and listened to some of the comments, which were moderated by Pastor Mullins, who allowed everyone who wished to plea their cases against the business venture to speak. As a member of Jasper's Elected Officials, Sheriff Hopkins chose to side with the community instead of the mayor on their petition, which adherently drew a bigger wedge between both men, hence Jonathan felt betrayed.

"I personally believe that if Mayor Becket aims to give out business permits like this, we should get us a new mayor," a female resident indicated!

"I agree with Miss Hines, Jasper ain't that type a town! Since Mayor Becket took office, we been getting all sort a indecent people here in town," another female stated!

"We can't become some prominent city without the railroad passing through Jasper, so Mayor Becket's vision for our town got no way to succeed," a male resident stated from his seat!

"We got a well respected and modest Christian community here, so allowing these types a businesses gonna ruin our good name! I can't imagine the types of ungodly and vulgar people who are gonna come live in our fair town," another male resident stood and said, which sent the audience into a frenzy!

"Settle down everyone, settle down! Now folks we are only here to get Mayor Becket to reconsider issuing this here unwelcomed business permit, and keep our town as it has always been," Pastor Mullins lamented!

Mayor Becket rose from his seat with his hat at hand, at which the audience members grew silent.

"We may not have the railroad passing through Jasper, but everybody knows we get our fair share of stagecoaches, settlers, and prospectors passing through town. Trust me when I say, not because we allow certain types of business our town is gonna change! We have the greatest lawman around for miles in Sheriff Hopkins, and if necessary, I am sure added revenue to the town will allow us to hire more deputes. I know many of you prefer living in a quiet community, but unless we start creating more work round these parts, all your kids are gonna grow up and move off to some bigger city, then Jasper will be a ghost town," the mayor declared!

Despite Jonathan's reasoning the citizens turned bias against him and began chanting, "bring back Mayor Rolley!"

The Mayor withdrew a cigar from his inner jacket pocket and sparked a match off his leather belt to set it ablaze, while the audience continued calling for Mayor Rolley's reinstatement. After Jonathan ensured that his cigar was properly lit, he raised his right hand to quiet the rowdy crowd, hence, everyone stopped their jeers and allowed him to speak.

"Now, how many jobs have Old Boy Rolley created since he been Mayor," Jonathan questioned?

Everyone in the crowd remained silent, knowing that their former mayor never opened any new enterprises.

"My plans will get at least a hundred of y'all steady work within a year! If Pastor Mullins over here can put food on y'all's table, maybe y'all should just vote for him instead," Becket argued!

Jonathan went over to his wife and took her hand into his, at which she stood up from her seat. The audience members began mumbling among themselves, before they turned to their host, and stared at him with disgust. The mayor's words resonated in the minds of many citizens, who realized he was trying to make their town prosperous, therefore, the meeting abruptly adjourned with everyone somewhat furious at Pastor Mullins. The Beckets walked down the isle toward the hall doors, where their gun-hands rejoined them at the weapon's counter, prior to leaving.

Mayor Becket's resentment toward Sheriff Hopkins reached its boiling point at that junction, therefore, he started devising ways to get rid of the lawman, without being considered the villain. Jasper's sheriff was hired by his predecessor, but the lawman had to be instated by the Governor of The State, so the town would have to hold an election for him to be replaced. As soon as Jonathan uncovered what was required for him to get rid of Sheriff Hopkins, he went into work a week later and filed the documents to host an election.

Before Mayor Becket filed the legal documents, he first had to find a challenger who stood a chance versus Sheriff Hopkins. The Jasper lawman was a popular figure in town, so everybody respected him. Most of the mayor's personal guards were despised by the local town folks, therefore, it would be a tough sledding with any of their names on the ballot. Jonathan was unsure who could challenge Sheriff Hopkins, until Beth told him who to assign. Following Beth's instruction, Jonathan summoned Jeff McCall, who was the most intellect of his gunners. Jeff was surprised he got offered the position, despite being the least fierce gunner among the guards. The day of the election was four months after the process was declared, so they had to convince the town's folks of his qualification within that time.

A month before the Sheriff's Election an unforeseen occurrence transpired, where three men broke into Jasper's Local Bank and robbed it. Although nobody was injured during the robbery, Sean McRay, Steve McRay, and Henry Bitts, who were outlaws from Texas, made away with over four thousand dollars. While escaping through town, the robbers fired several shots at citizens outside the bank, that send patrons racing for safety. After Sheriff Hopkins got informed of the robbery, he decided to form a posse and chased after the thieves, who were heading south. Most of the men were scared to go after the infamous McRay gang, so Jonathan volunteered three of his trusted gunners to help with the manhunt. Sheriff Hopkins desperately needed assistance, therefore, he accepted the mayor's offer without suspicion.

Jonathan pulled Quick Draw to the side before the posse left and gave him final instructions. "Make sure you kill Hopkins before you gets back here, and make it look like an accident!"

"You got it boss," Quick Draw responded!

Sheriff Hopkins rode out of town with a nine men posse and left Deputy Eli Marks to uphold the law. Sean McRay and his associates exited town seventeen-minutes before the manhunt team's departure, therefore, their horse tracks were fresh and easily identified. The bandits expected they would have gotten followed, so they rode hard to cross state's line, knowing the town's lawmen had jurisdictions.

Sean McRay was the leader of their gang and the most skilled with his pistol. Both he and his best friend Henry Bitts had been getting in trouble since they were little boys, before they began involving his younger brother Steve. After riding for miles without seeing any lawmen, the bandits assumed they had gotten away safely, therefore, they found a location to set up camp for the night. The ten men posse chased after the thieves relentlessly and caught up to them later that evening. The thieves were preparing their supper, while they counted, and shared the money they stole.

The sheriff and his temporarily deputized cowboys found the bandits' camp just before dusk, but decided to wait until dark before they moved in. They abandoned their horses almost a hundred metres from the thieves' camp, then went the rest of the way on foot. Quick Draw and Mr. Becket's other two gunhands brought along their rifles, while the other cowboys followed the sheriff's lead and relied solely on their side pistols. After they made their way through brushes and pointy twigs, the cowboys came upon the robbers' camp, where they first hid and surveyed the bunch. The decision was made to separate into two teams, which should have allowed them to easily capture the thieves without incident.

Sheriff Hopkins thought they all shared the same objectives, and thus perceived nothing suspicious when the mayor's guards all associated themselves with the other group. The sheriff gave his supporting cast strict instructions on how they would proceed, before the group of deputies went off. Quick Draw and the others made their way along the edge of the woods, until they were almost parallel to the sheriff. With their apprehension plot devised, the posse members snuck into position and remained hidden in the bushes, until Brad shouted out and made their presence known.

"This is Sheriff Hopkins from Jasper! You men are all under arrest for robbing our local bank earlier today! Now before you fellows get all antsy, I want y'all to know that I got some other deputes across yonder in them bushes! So, toss away them guns and stand up where we can see y'all clear, with your hands high in the air," Sheriff Hopkins threatened!

As soon as the sheriff began speaking, Sean grabbed the pot of coffee and poured in on the fire, before they laid flat on their stomachs in the dirt, with their firearms at the ready. It became incredibly dark around the camp site, yet the thieves looked around and tried to determine who exactly they were up against. There was the possibility that their intruder could have been a lone vigilante, so Sean tried to get more clarification before they made their next move. The three bank robbers hid behind the huge boulders in the camp site, which offered them some protection against their antagonists.

"You got the wrong people sheriff, we ain't robbed no bank," Sean yelled!

"Son, we been tracking y'all all day! Now we fitting to bring y'all back, alive, or dead, it makes no difference to me," Sheriff Hopkins responded!

"Like I said sheriff, we ain't robbed no bank! So, unless you want trouble, you best ride on out of here," Sean declared!

None of the bandits were willing to simply surrender, therefore, they were prepared to shoot it out and tried their luck. Instead of a vocal response, a single shot rang out from the location where the voice sounded, before an eruption of gunfire unfolded. Henry Bitts and his companions thought the sheriff was lying about 'having associates in the adjacent woods,' therefore, they disregarded the threat. As gunshots rang out, the McRay brothers returned fire, yet kept their heads lowered to avoid being struck. To get a clearer shot at one of their antagonists, Henry raised his head slightly higher than his partners. Quick Draw took the opportunity and shot Henry directly through the back, which clarified the warning previously given by the sheriff.

With one third of their gang eliminated, Steve and Sean immediately looked to escape, and tried crawling away from there location. Instead of following Sean directly, Steve first rolled over toward the sac with the stolen money, but got shot in the abdomen while retrieving it. Unlike Sean whose main concern was escaping and thus moved towards their horses, Steve was not about to neglect the money regardless of their situation. To keep the lawmen at bay, the injured bandit fired two shots in either direction, as he crawled through the dirt behind his brother.

The second bullet that struck the lingering bank robber penetrated his back and damaged his lower spine, thereby, he dropped the money sac and grabbed for the wound, as he winced in pain. Sean did not fare any better than his sibling, after the first bullet struck him in the thigh. The gang leader was successfully making it to his horse, until one of the riflemen shot him in the rib. Despite being seriously injured, Steve continued crawling and reached Sean's bootheels. Even though both brothers had wounded, they were still defiant and found the strength to shoot back at the deputized lawmen.

The dark made it incredibly difficult for the cowboys to get clear shot. Both thieves crawled a short distance from their original camping ground, under immense pressure from their antagonists. Sean's pair of Colt 38mm Special handguns ran out of bullets and placed their escape in jeopardy, as he was unable to reload under the circumstance. Even though the lawmen clearly had the advantage, they cautiously advanced from their hiding places, to stop the thieves before they reached their horses. With the decrease in returned gunfire, Sheriff Hopkins stepped from behind the tree that protected him and began moving forward. The deputes who stayed with him also moved out into the open and began advancing toward the desperate criminals.

"I ain't gonna tell you boys to surrender again," Sheriff Hopkins called out to the bandits!

"Alright, stop shooting, we give up," Sean shouted!

"Well then toss them guns over yonder," Sheriff Hopkins instructed!

Jethrow realized that they stood no chance of escaping and threw his guns aside, then reached into his vest's inner pocket for his Flask of Whiskey. While retrieving the liquor container to partake of a drink, Junior who was grouped with Quick Draw's team yelled out from in the bushes. "Watch it Sheriff," before he shot and killed Sean! The Sheriff took his eyes off the thieves and spun around to enquire the reason for shooting, by using hand gestures.

"Sorry Sheriff, it looked like he had a gun," Junior exclaimed!

With the sheriff's attention focused on Junior, Steve shook his brother's leg and realized his idol had been killed. The outraged bandit spun onto his back with his weapon pointed in the sheriff's direction. Brad spun back around to the most frightening sighting of his career, with Steve's shaking hand aiming his Remington 38mm handgun at him. The sheriff clinched his eyelids shut tight, fearing he would get struck as two shots discharged from the thief's weapon.

Quick Draw and another temporarily deputized help from across the bushes where Beckets' guards were positioned, also discharged their weapon. Everybody was stunned by the developments, therefore, they looked anticipation to see who had gotten shot. Easton Quids, who was one of the deputies behind Sheriff Hopkins tumbled to the ground, before Brad also succumbed to his injury and dropped dead.

"He just shot Sheriff Hopkins," Quick Draw lamented after Steve's lifeless hand also dropped to the ground!

Some of the men raced to check on the sheriff who had no pulse and was declared dead by Walter Hedges. Upon inspection of the gunshot wound, Walter thought it was impossible for Steve who was on the ground, directly ahead of the sheriff, to have shot him in the chest. The bullet penetrated from a higher trajectory and went directly through Brad, instead of travelling upward from someone who was flat against his back. Walter looked off in the direction from which the shot could have originated, and saw Quick Draw viciously staring at him, while he replaced the spent bullets into his rifle. The cowboys spent the night at the bandit's campsite, then returned to Jasper the following morning with the recovered money, and the deceased bodies.

CHAPTER
THIRTEEN

Walking Turtle taught both Coyote and Nicco everything
he knew about their fathers, from they were old enough
to understand their native tongue. Even though the boys
considered him their father, Walking Turtle instilled in them
that he was their honored stepfather, in memory of his dear
friends. The boys were taught to wrestle, grapple, and fight at a young age, and
would often spar against each other during training. Unlike most of the village
children, the dark and red complexion brothers who had no issues with their
different skin colors, were shooting arrows and tossing knives as soon as they
developed the strength to handle such weapons.

Although the boys considered Walking Turtle their father, he held a memo-
rial ceremony each year on the day of their biological fathers' killing, to hon-
or them. Both Nicco and Coyote bared striking resemblance to their fathers,
which was a comment they heard from Walking Turtle regularly. Neither of
the boys were given any specific treatment over the other, therefore, Walking
Turtle taught them to the best of his ability. The biracial brothers were also
taught the powers of healing and the usage of herbs to cure one's ailments.

Coyote and Nicco had similar interests and matching personalities, but the
African descendant had a special gift with animals. From a young age, Coyote would bring insects and rodents into the family's teepee, and had to be
searched by Walking Turtle every time he entered, to ensure he did not have
any creatures with him. He would care for injured reptiles and animals like
no other native, and was said to have the ability to speak with the creatures

with which he interacted. If Coyote was not on some expedition with Nicco, it was guaranteed that he would be found meddling with wild creature off the campgrounds.

For three consecutive years Shushuni carried babies for her new partner, however, each time she gave birth the couple got blessed with girls. The first of the three females were Shadaiia, followed by Yazieka, and finally Kuzuri. Instead of developing any resentments for not getting his biological sons, Walking Turtle grew and taught his daughters like he would any other son. Due to the girls' upbringing, they all grew to become three of the fiercest females throughout the village, thereby, they were never reluctant to accept any challenge from either sex.

Many of the other mothers in the village questioned Walking Turtle's methods of raising his daughters and would often comment to Shushuni. Following that night where their village got attacked by the cowboys, Shushuni witnessed so much bloodshed, that she supported her partner's training. Shushuni rather than Walking Turtle wanted for all her children to become self-sufficient, to the extent she insisted they practiced, rather than played games.

Like their fathers before them, Nicco and Coyote left the village often to explore their surroundings, and would travel for miles. They would be gone for hours before they returned, yet Walking Turtle was never concerned about their wellbeing. The Cherokee lived off the land by a certain code of conduct, that was passed down through generations. Native Indians predominately remembered what their ancestors lost to the white, so many restrictions were placed on the children to keep them from integrating with Caucasians.

The first time both boys unintentionally slept away from the village and broke camp rules, they were nine years of age, and tried to follow the river as far as they safely could. To begin their exploration, they made Stick Boats using small pieces of tree balk, with wide leaves stuck in the middle that served as sails. They both set their boats to race in the water, then followed along on the bank while they raced downstream. It was customary for anyone leaving the village to carry some sort of protection, therefore, both boys walked with spears. After nearly than an hour of pursuit, the young explorers realized they were well beyond their targeted destination, and sought to return home. As they looked around their surroundings to determine exactly where they were, everything appeared foreign, before a strange sound emitted from the forest behind them.

Coyote was never bothered by weird animal sounds, therefore, he walked off from his brother to investigate the cause. "My boat win race, your boat too slow," stated Coyote as he walked away!

"Brother come on, we must return," Nicco answered!

Nicco hesitated for a while, then turned to follow Coyote. A huge Cougar blindsided the young Indian, when it charged from the forest and knocked him to the ground. The animal leapt onto Nicco from the left side and bit him along the base of the neck and upper left shoulder. The protective spear Nicco carried fell from his hand, therefore, without an alternative weapon he was at the animal's mercy. With his brother unaware of his predicament Nicco squealed as loudly as he could, which was all that he could have done defensively. Once the third-generation African Indian observed his sibling being mauled, he attacked with his spear and threw it like a javelin into the Cougar neck. The critically injured animal instantly withdrew its fangs from Nicco's neck, and staggered about growling until it crashed to the ground.

"Please forgive me mighty beast," whispered Coyote to the Cougar as he ran by to his brother's aide!

Despite the guilt felt by the animal lover for killing the cougar, he was more concerned about Nicco's health, and thus applied pressure to the wound. Blood continued pouring from the wound, so Coyote did his best to reduce to bleeding. Walking Turtle had taught them enough survival skills to help them regardless of their situation, therefore, Coyote looked around for anything that might be useful.

"Help me, brother," Coyote muffled!

There was a hermit known as Jikaranchi, who lived nearby in a cottage with his wolf dog named Savage. Jikaranchi was a half Cherokee, half Caucasian male, who lived in solitary after he was shunned by the white folks in the town of Jasper, where he grew up. The hermit's mother was a Cherokee female who got sold into a life of servitude as a child, before her caretaker raped her and thus produced him. During his mother's pregnancy, his biological father threatened to kill them both if she ever made any claim of him being the father. Despite an immaculate resemblance to his father, Jikaranchi was never accepted by his Caucasians family members, and got seen more as an outsider by the Native Indians. Both Jikaranchi and his rescued pet were inside his residence when the dog overheard Coyote's alerts and began barking.

"What is it boy," Jikaranchi asked, to which the dog went to the door and started spinning around?

Jikaranchi grabbed his Winchester Rifle and tied a leach around Savage's neck to prevent the dog from running away, while he followed his trusted pet to investigate whatever caused the disruptive behavior. Upon arrival Jikaranchi was surprised to find two Indian boys by themselves and thought there was something suspicious. Instead of rushing in to investigate, the hermit remained hidden in the shadows of the trees, and watched to ensure it was not a trap. Following his visual diagnosis, Jikaranchi determined that the young Indians were possibly attacked by the dead cougar.

"Hello, I am Jikaranchi! My dog hear you calling out... I am only here to help you," introduced the Hermit speaking the Cherokee language, while he approached with caution!

"How you know to talk Cherokee," asked Coyote who was surprised to see and hear a Caucasian type male speaking his native language?

The decision to accept Jikaranchi's help was then made quite easily by Coyote, who knew the danger his brother was in. Prior to examining the injured child, Jikaranchi unfastened his dog's leach and allowed the animal to roam about and provided security. Once Jikaranchi checked Nicco's wound, he quickly scooped the boy up and hurried back to his cottage. When they reached the dwelling, Jikaranchi made Coyote continued applying pressure, until he cleaned and dressed the wounds. The half Indian boiled some herbs on his wooden fire and gave Nicco a cup of warm tea. Coyote keenly watched everything that Jikaranchi did for Nicco, while Savage drew close to the African Indian's leg and went to sleep.

*

Late that night Shushuni could not sleep a wink with her sons away from the Cherokee village. Her partner was sound asleep knowing he had taught his sons to survive on their own. After Shushuni ran out of patience, she awoke Walking Turtle and sent him out to find their sons. Walking Turtle gathered a small group of hunters and went out in search of the young lads. After an hour of searching with the help of torches, the men returned to the village emptyhanded. Shushuni was frantic with worry and stayed up that entire night in front of their hut, jumping at the slightest sound while hoping each time it was her sons. Among the family members, Walking Turtle was the only person confident they would return home safely, nevertheless, he could not sleep a wink either.

As soon as the light of the sun brightened the plains, a group of searchers left the village to locate their missing children. Shadaiia helped to point the search party in the right direction, when she confessed that, "she watched her brothers walked toward the river when they departed!" Eagle Sight who was the village's best tracker found the boys' tracks and followed them along the riverbank for approximately forty minutes. As they advanced along the riverbed, Eagle Sight suddenly stopped, then signalled his companions to hide. At the tracker's instructions, his companions began climbing trees and finding other hiding places. There were people approaching and the tracker had no idea who they were, thus, for precautionary reasons he instructed the group to conceal themselves. The Cherokee trackers had no idea who approached; therefore, everyone readied their weapons to strike.

The Cherokee search party was on a collision course with Jikaranchi and his dog Savage, who were transporting Nicco and Coyote back to their village. Jikaranchi had Nicco on his back, to help conserve his strength during the long trip. As they approached the area where the search party members found illusive places to conceal themselves, Coyote grabbed onto Jikaranchi's hand and stopped him before he walked into a clearing. Savage began barking to indicate there was danger ahead, therefore, everyone grew concerned for their lives. Without uttering a word Coyote stooped down to one knee, lowered himself to the ground, as he stared high up a tree, and sniffed the air like a dog.

"We must go back! There is ambushers in the bushes; and in those trees! Look there," Coyote whispered!

"How can you be so sure, I see no one," Jikaranchi argued?!

Coyote had been taught to master the skills of the warrior from an early age, so he had an excellent sense of smell, and remarkable vision. The young warrior sensed that the hidden Indians might be friendlies, therefore, he tried to distinguish who they were.

"Whit-whit-whit," Coyote whistled!

"Whit-whit-woo," Walking Turtle responded!

The young African American Indian stood back upright, then confidently proceeded ahead the instant he received the confirmation. The half Cherokee, half Caucasian male was not taught the ways of the Indian warrior as a child, therefore, he did not have the skills which the boys possessed. Jikaranchi was surprised when the people who Coyote spoke of began emerging from their hiding places.

Every member of the search party felt elated when they saw Coyote, dragging the dead cougar on a wooden pulling sled. Walking Turtle hugged Coyote, then took Nicco from Jikaranchi and examined him. Coyote introduced the hermit to the villagers and told them about the help he provided them. Jikaranchi got invited to the Cherokee village for the first time, where he was welcomed with open arms by the community.

CHAPTER
FOURTEEN

News of Jasper's revised laws against gambling and prostitution enticed many opportunistic business people to relocate. There were either thrill seekers or new residents, arriving by stagecoaches and other means, almost every other day. The new influx of settlers led to the constructions of new homes and businesses, which expanded the town's landscape. Gold miners were still flocking to the area, even though no one else had managed to find any of the precious mineral.

With such a lucrative market, criminals also flocked to the town, with aspirations of making a quick buck. However, word had circulated about the McRay Gang's demise, so visitors were extremely cautious. Mayor Becket was determined to have his form of law and order governed the town, therefore, the rules changed drastically.

Moments after Sheriff Hopkins' body got returned, Jonathan walked to the jailhouse with a pair of his gun hands, to speak with Deputy Marks regarding the open position. The deputy was in the process of releasing a sobered-up prisoner, when Quick Draw opened the door for his boss to enter, then locked it behind them. Jonathan entered and knocked the ashes from his cigar onto the floor, then placed it between his lips.

"Ah Mayor-Mayor Becket, I'll, I'll, I'll be right with you sir," stuttered Deputy Marks!

The prisoner who was being released got handed his gun belt, and buckled it around his waist, then picked up the rest of his belongings off the desk.

"Earl I gotta issue you a two dollar fine for pissing on the sidewalk last night and breaking Mister Hawley's window," Deputy Marks declared!

"Ah come on Eli, I was drunk," Earl pled before he took out the money and paid the fine! "Anyways, thanks for getting me somewhere safe to sleep off that liquor! See you around... Mayor!"

Both men tipped their hats to each other as the prisoner walked by and exited the jailhouse. Mayor Becket went over to the Sheriff's desk and took a seat, as he continued puffing on his cigar.

"What can I do for you Mayor," Deputy Marks asked?

"It's a damn shame what happened to Old Boy Hopkins! But then again in your line a business, I'm sure you understand that's what comes with the territory, especially when you don't follow my orders," Mayor Becket threatened!

"I, I, I don't know what you talking about," Deputy Marks answered!

"Your boss the sheriff was killed last night! They just rolled his body and them bank robbers in a few minutes ago," Mayor Becket stated!

The deputy looked around shocked, as if he was unsure what to do next, before he said, "I, I, I guess, I could be sheriff!"

"Now, I really don't think you got the skills to be sheriff, but you damn sure got the temperament for the job! Given the types of visitors passing through Jasper lately, I believe we need someone far better at handling a firearm! Sheriff Hopkins was about to lose his job in the upcoming election anyway, so we'll just go ahead and make Jim McCall here, our next sheriff," Mayor Becket exclaimed, as he puffed on his cigar!

"You, you, you the mayor so I guess, whatever you feel is right! I, I, I'll backup Sheriff McCall and help him keep our town safe," Deputy Marks declared!

"I guess the only thing we need to do now is get the governor here to certify our new sheriff. Here you go Sheriff McCall, lets see how that badge looks on you," Mayor Becket instructed as he tossed his gun hand the badge!

Jim McCall caught the badge and pinned it to his leather vest. Mayor Becket felt proud seeing one of his personal employees wearing the sheriff's badge, as he stood up and walked toward the front door. Quick Draw opened the door for his boss, who continued puffing away on his cigar.

"With this town getting as big as it is, I think we may need to hire a new deputy! You fellows might as well put up a sign in the window for new deputy," Jonathan ordered before he left the jailhouse!

Sheriff Jim McCall walked over to the desk and sat in his chair. Eli went and cleaned up the cell in which Earl slept, before he attended to the wanted sign. After he got through writing up the deputy wanted sign, Eli was about to place it in the window, when a settler busted in through the door.

"Where is the Sheriff," asked the settler, before he saw Jim sitting behind the desk?

"Sheriff Hopkins was killed last night, trying to bring to justice a band of bank robbers! This here is Sheriff McCall and I'm his deputy, what can we do for you," Eli stated?

"Howdy Sheriff McCall! Me, my two kids, and my wife Esmerelda was relocating to this here fair town a yours, when a few miles out, we came up on a crashed wagon! The three people aboard appeared to have been robbed and killed, but there was one fellow who was still breathing, even though he had been shot up pretty bad! We brought him over to Doc Withers, who is trying to patch him up, but the Doc warned me to run over and tell y'all what happened," said the settler!

"Let's head over to Doc Withers' office and see if we can find out anything, in case this fellow dies! What do they call you," Sheriff McCall stated?

"I'm Peter Green sheriff," the man answered!

"Pleased to meet you Peter," Jim exclaimed!

"Likewise, sheriff," Peter responded!

Doctor Frank Withers was the town's seventy-year-old physician, who had a section attached to his house, where he practiced medicine. By the time Jim and Eli arrived by Doc Withers' office, the physician was pulling the last of five bullets from the male patient. The doctor's wife Helene attended to the door, then led the new sheriff and his deputy into the room where the operation was ongoing. The lawmen hoped they would be able to ask the patient a few questions, that might provide some answers, but the unidentified male was unconscious and still in critical condition. Doc Withers was amazed that the patient was still alive, after being shot several times, and highlighted where each bullet penetrated. Following the operation, the Doc could only be optimistic about the man's chances of survival, although he leaned more toward a positive outcome.

The man survived and awakened two days later, frightened, and surprised that he was still breathing. Helene Withers was alone at her husband's medical practice facility, when his patient awoke screaming at someone. "Stop, don't shoot," yelled the patient before he opened his eyes screaming! The sudden outcry made Helene raced into the room, where the patient was startled when she entered. The pain from the man's wounds restricted his movements, and caused tremendous anguish, but there was very little Helene could do.

Despite his predicament, a minute later the patient tried rolling off the bed, to get back on his feet. It was obvious that the patient had other places to be, but Helene had to stop him before he caused more damage to himself. She did her best to make him comfortable by wiping his sweat, feeding him water, and fixing his blanket.

"Take it easy cowboy, you ain't quite healed up yet," Helene instructed.

"Where am I," asked the patient?

"You in the Town of Jasper! You been here for two days now," Helene answered.

"What happened to the people, I was with," struggled to ask the patient?

"From what I heard, the two people found dead were laid to rest yesterday, if those the folks you talking about!? I believe the sheriff was looking to speak with you regarding who did that to y'all," Helene stated!

"Kindly inform your sheriff, there ain't no need for that talk, cause, I got a bad memory at describing people," lamented the patient!

"What is your name if you don't mind me asking," Helene asked?

"I'm sorry ma-am, in all my rage I forgot ma manners, thank you for saving my life! My name is Gus Blank, and those two people killed was my sister Sue Blank, and her son Ben. We sold everything we had to move west, and them thieves took it all," the patient somberly said.

"Well, I'm truly sorry for your lost and hope they find whoever done this," Helene said!

Aside from dealing with the drunks in town and maintaining the peace, the murdered settlers became the lawmen's biggest legal issue to solve. Such atrocities went against everything Mayor Becket was building; therefore, he wanted those responsible found. With the next town located over a hundred miles away, the lawmen knew that those responsible were most likely still in the vicinity. To solve the case, once Sheriff McCall got word that the patient was awake, Deputy Marks and he visited the recovering male. When they spoke with Gus, he failed to provide much physical description, because the bandits covered their faces with bandanas. The recovering patient however, described how many bandits were involved, and what they stole.

Gus Blank was back on his feet and out of bed a few days later, primarily due to Mrs. Withers who insisted he spent at lease a week healing, before he was allowed to do anything strenuous. The elderly yet comfort warming doctor's aide, treated Gus with such kindness that he felt compelled to obey her wishes. He spent several hours at the cemetery following his departure, where he mourned and spoke to his dead relatives.

Despite all the medical help provided, Doc Withers offered Gus a temporary place to stay until he made some money and decided what was his next move. With only the clothes on his back in his possession, Gus accepted the Doc's offer and vowed to repay everything he owed. There were minor repairs around the doctor's residence that needed attention, therefore, Gus went around and fixed the roof, a few windows, and even helped Helene in her garden.

Once Gus became healthy enough for more strenuous activities, he went out in search of a job. There were several men in town who did not wear gun belts, but without his tied to his thighs, Gus felt uneased as he walked through town. After enquiring at a number of businesses, Gus decided to seek employment at Becket's Hardware Store, and walked over to the building. Two of Mayor Becket's guard were outside the store smoking cigarettes, and scrupulously looked at the job seeker as he walked by. Without any visible weapons neither guard thought of him as a threat, and, allowed him to freely enter the store. Inside the establishment Mayor Becket was having a discussion with Lester Jones, who was one of the prosperous businessmen in town.

Gus stepped to one of the employees behind the counter, and asked about acquiring a job, but was told 'there were no openings.' Undeterred by the response, he walked from the store and stepped out onto the adjoined side porch. Directly across the street, the three men who robbed and killed Gus' family members dismounted off their horses. Despite being unable to physically identify the thieves, Gus recognized the horses, his personal gun belt being worn by one of the robbers, and his sister's handkerchief. The three robbers were laughing and ramping among themselves, as they walked into the Saloon, where a flock of whores surrounded and welcomed them.

Gus rushed back into the hardware store and went directly for the weapon's showcase. The employee who attended to him before, walked over to offer him assistance.

"What can I do for you this time sir," Warren asked?

"Listen to me, I was shot five times and left for dead! My sister and nephew got shot and killed at the same time; and the men who did the killing, just walked into that there saloon across the street! Please, I'm begging you to loan me a pistol and three bullets, and I swear I'll pay you back once I recover some of the stuff they stole from me," Gus pled?

"I'm terribly sorry---" began Warren, before Mayor Becket overheard the conversation and interrupted!

"Those guns can't be sold new after they been fired now can they… But if you wish, I will loan you the one off my hip," Mayor Becket offered?

"I graciously accept your offer sir," Gus answered without hesitation, at which Jonathan removed his gun belt and gave it to him!

Gus took the belt and fastened it around his waist, then withdrew the Colt 45 Calibre, and checked to ensure there were bullets inside the chambers. With his body not yet at a hundred percent, Gus winced as he extended his right hand and formed a fist with his fingers tight.

"Maybe you ought to leave this until you healthy enough," Mayor Becket declared?

"You, run across the road into the saloon and tell the three men who just entered, that someone they buried came back from hell to say hello," Gus instructed the younger employee, who took off running!

The employee ran across the street into the saloon where he had never been. The young man was astonished by the sexual atmosphere, as whores brought their customers up and down the stairs. There were half naked women parading about the saloon, while they behaved provocatively in the open. The establishment was festive with someone playing the piano, loud conversations, and a singer performing. As he gazed forward, the hardware store employee bumped into the waitress, who almost overturned her liquor tray.

"Is you drunk or something, look where you going," argued the waitress?!

"I'm sorry, but I have a message for the three men who just walked in," said the employee, at which the waitress pointed out two men over by the bar!

One of the men playing Poker noticed when the waitress pointed to his comrades, so he stood up from his seat, and walked across to the bar. The scared young man slowly walked over to the bar, where the bandits noticed him approaching. The men seated by the bar first pushed away the whores leaning on them, before they stood up and rested their hands closer to their weapons.

"I have a message for you," the employee stated.

"And what is the message," Bobba demanded?

"Some man inside the hardware store, said to tell you fine gentlemen, 'that you buried him, and he came back from hell to say hello,' declared the young man before he ran out of the saloon!

Kyle, Bobba, and Happi angrily exited the saloon and immediately took note of a man standing a few paces away, in the middle of the street. At first none of the accused thieves knew who the man was, until they stepped onto the road and got a better view of his face.

"It seems you got a problem dying, but we don't mind killing you twice," threatened Happi as they moved side by side towards Gus, then stopped approximately twenty yards away!

"I'm gonna give all three a you the chance none of you gave me or my sister... Draw them guns whenever y'all ready," Gus challenged!

People along the street and sidewalks began racing for cover, knowing that once a quarrel got to that stage, someone was about to die. The four men stood ready to duel with a crowd of spectators' eager to see the outcome. Despite their eagerness, each spectator hid behind whatever protective barriers they could find, to avoid getting accidentally shot.

The cowboys stood in a stare down for approximately twenty seconds, until total silence drowned out the noise. Happi began getting antsy and started reaching for his holstered pistol first. Gus pulled out his borrowed Colt 45 and shot the three men square in the chest, twirled the gun on his index finger, and re-holstered it, before Bobba and Kyle could even extract their weapons.

Happi managed to pull his firearm from the holster and fired a shot into the ground, before he succumbed to his injury. Gus walked over to the dead men and removed Kyle's gun belt, confiscated the monies from their pockets, and reclaimed whatever belonged to his family members.

"Click-click," sounded Sheriff McCall's shotgun, as he stood on the sidewalk aiming at Gus. "You better have a mighty good reason for killing those men," threatened the sheriff!

"This is my gun belt, and that black stallion over yonder is also mine, you can check my initials is on the saddle! And these the thieves who killed my sister and nephew," Gus explained as he kicked Bobba on the leg!

Mayor Becket was highly impressed with Gus' skill with a pistol and recalled him enquiring about a job. Jonathan walked over with his gun hands by his side, at which Gus handed him his firearm.

"Thank you kindly mister," Gus said!

"You loaned him your gun Mayor," Sheriff McCall questioned?

"What is your name stranger," enquired Mayor Becket?

"I'm Gus Blank! You really the mayor," Gus stated?

"In the flesh Mr. Blank. I'd like to know if you would be interested in being our new town deputy? We surely could use a gun hand with your talents," Mayor Becket asked!

Gus looked directly into the mayor's eyes, then took a few seconds to look around his surrounding. He had retrieved his double pistol holster, his horse, and some of his stolen money, therefore, he was not desperately in need of the job. The position being offered was indeed deadly and challenging, but Gus thought about some of the heartwarming folks he had met in town. With his relatives buried in their cemetery, Gus also considered being abled to visit their graves, therein, he accepted the offer.

CHAPTER
FIFTEEN

Nicco, Coyote, Shadaiia, and Maharuk were all around the average age of thirteen, when they decided to go out horse trapping. Coyote found a section by the river where a herd of wild horses went to drink and sometimes bathed. The four native youths hid in the tall bushes down wind, along the trail used by the horses, and waited until the herd showed up for their daily drink. Shadaiia joined forces with her bigger brother Coyote to catch one horse, while Nicco paired with Maharuk to catch another.

To catch the horses the trappers made lassos, to rope the animals they selected around their necks. After a long wait and numerous debates about leaving, the Indians detected the horses coming from listening to the ground. The Alpha Horse first came into view at the top of a ridge, where he scouted their water spot to ensure it was clear. Seconds later the rest of the herd joined him before they all descended to the river.

"Nicco, I believe our fathers capture Tornado from this herd," Coyote whispered!

"Yeah, you might be right. But that spotted brown and white coat is mine," Nicco whispered!

"The white horse is mine," Coyote instructed as they watched the horses cautiously walk down to the river, where they eventually shed their fears, and played around freely!

With the horses bathing in the river, the youngsters crawled closer to their targets, which had no idea Indians were in the vicinity. There was a slight distance from the edge of the tall bushes to the river, so unless the trappers timed their attack perfectly, they would have lost all the horses. When they reached the edge of the grass, the Alpha Horse suspected something foul, therefore, the animal raised its head and began looking around. The lead horse looked around until he was satisfied there was no danger, after which he calmed down and went back to watching the herd.

The perfect time to attack came when both the horses chosen started playing around in depths of deeper water. Both teams of Indians rushed the herd, but only caught four horses still in the river. Nicco first lassoed his choice at the edge of the river, then began tussling with the animal to gain control, while Maharuk also firmly held the rope. The white horse chosen by Coyote began running behind the other two horses, as they tried to escape down river. Once he got the opportunity, the African American Indian also lassoed his choice, which wanted to escape with its herd.

The rest of the herd ran away from the situation behind their alpha leader, whose primary duty was to keep them all safe regardless of the losses sustained. Nicco's brown and white spotted horse fought to join its fleeing companions, none of which could have done anything to assist with its dilemma. In comparison to the young trappers, the horses with whom they tussled were mammoth creatures, nevertheless, the self-sufficient youths handled them like their adult counterparts. Both Maharuk and Nicco held firmly onto the lasso around their horse's neck and maintained a slight distance, while the animal kicked with its front hoofs and fought for them to release the rope.

Coyote and his sister Shadaiia were fortunate to lasso their horse while the animal was still in the river, where the elements made it much easier for them to get him settled. The beautiful white colored young stallion initially put up a huge struggle, until Coyote used his horse whispering technique to calm him. The colored Indian lowered his head in submission and walked slowly towards the wild animal, with his palms exposed. Years of interaction with wild creatures have taught Coyote how to correspond with them, so he strangely spoke in context that the horse understood and responded. Once Coyote got close enough to the horse, he withdrew an apple from a pouch around his waist and fed it to the animal.

Neither Nicco nor Maharuk who both maintained a firm grip on the rope around their horse's neck, could believe that Coyote had already broken his wild stallion. Both Indians were the first to lasso their horse, yet were still struggling to calm the feisty animal. Following a short engagement process, Coyote adjusted the rope around his horse's neck, then leapt aboard the powerful stallion. The animal lover rode up and down the riverside, as if the horse and he were old acquaintance.

Coyote returned and jumped off the horse, then allowed Shadaiia to climb aboard and ride about, while he assisted his brother. Every Indian was taught to ride horses from a very young age; therefore, the female handled the animal as well as any of her siblings. Nicco's horse showed no signs of tiring as it continued tussling to escape, until Coyote used the same technique he did on his mount, to calm the wild mammal. With their objectives attained, the four young Indians rode about the open plains and thoroughly enjoyed the fruits of their labor, before they contemplated returning home.

Shadaiia wanted to pick some Red Berries, so she and their mother could prepare her favorite spiced dough. Nicco and Coyote had toured the vast regions that surrounded their village, therefore, they brought her to a place that was abundant with berries. The Red Berry Patch was several miles away from their village, along the side of a hill, just beyond a back trail that was often used by travellers. There had been much fewer robberies throughout the territory following the McCall gang, but people seldomly got robbed along that path. Nicco and Coyote had absolutely no interest in helping their sister pick berries, so they laid in the grass and watched their horses freely graze about. Maharuk had an undisclosed liking for Shadaiia, so he offered to assist with collecting the berries.

While their companions collected the Red Berries, Nicco laid in the grass and looked up at the blue sky. With his ears close to the ground, Nicco distinctively heard a wagon and a few horsemen approaching. The cautious Indian immediately warned Shadaiia and Maharuk, 'to get the horses and hide themselves!' The berry pickers retrieved the horses and ran deep into the wooded area, until they were summoned by the others. Both Coyote and Nicco also hid among the trees, but stayed closer to the edges, to observe what was happening. The young warriors watched as two men operating an open back wagon, covered with a tarp, met with four riders on horsebacks. The Indians had heard many stories about Caucasians, but they had never actually seen a white man. It was uncommon for anyone to do business out on the open plains, so the youngsters watched the suspicious meeting.

The two cowboys seated in the wagon's box, were liquor smugglers who sold their products to Jonathan Becket's newest business competitor, J.T. Pereau. Mister Pereau owned the Showcase Lounge, which highlighted stage performers with unique talents for the audience members. Following their transaction, the smugglers would meet with men employed by Mr. Pereau, who bought their goods in exchange for currency. However, on that occasion the smugglers had no idea the men with whom they met were scammers.

The mayor's son Horace Becket found out about the liquor arrangement from Dave Lexton, who was one of the men Mr. Pereau paid to collect his illegal liquor. Once Horace found out about the business deal and saw the opportunity to make some extra money, he told his troublesome friends about the deal. The four men on horseback were subsequently, Horace Becket, his two friends Jim Pigston and George Teague, along with Dave Lexton, whom the smugglers knew from prior dealings.

Dave Lexton was addicted to gambling Poker, but got drunk playing inside Becket's Saloon one night, before he began mouthing off about his new security gig. Horace was an ambitious eighteen-year-old, who had begun working for his father inside the saloon, when he overheard the drunken rant, which nobody else but him took seriously. Since that night Horace befriended Dave, then tricked him into believing that he should be earning much more money for his involvement in the liquor smuggling.

On the day of the next scheduled pickup, Horace and his two friends ambushed Dave and the other transporter, while they travelled to the designated location. Dave pretended as if he knew nothing of the thieves, who hijacked them several miles out of town. To conceal their deceit, George Teague shot Dave's partner dead the moment they rode up. With the funds secured, Horace and his band of scammers proceeded to the meeting location, where even though the smugglers knew Dave, they were somewhat suspicious.

"What happened to your other partner," the wagon driver asked?

"He couldn't make it," Horace answered!

"I was asking him," insinuated the driver, as he pointed at Dave!

Horace felt insulted and leaned forward in his saddle, before he rested his right hand on his gun handle, then turned to look back at Dave, who had began responding. With the smugglers' attention directed towards his associate, Horace unexpectedly withdrew his 38mm and shot both men. Nicco and Coyote were astonished by the killings, yet remained silent and continued watching, as Dave dismounted his horse, shoved the smugglers from the box, and took control of the reigns. After the gang of scammers departed, the young Indians went to check on the murdered cowboys, whose bodies were left for the birds and animals.

It was an old Indian custom to never desecrate the bodies of dead people, but given the opportunity to own their personal firearms, was something neither warrior could resist. The young misfits removed and confiscated the cowboys' Colt 45mm handguns and gun belts, even though they were not of age to own such items. Knowing the weapons would have been taken by their elders, the talented youths quickly dug a hole, wrapped the guns with a cloth, and buried them. To ensure that their secret remained as such, they decided against disclosing their findings to Shadaiia and Maharuk. Following their deceitful actions, Nicco and Coyote retrieved their associates, then exited in another direction, to prevent their colleagues from seeing the dead bodies.

The thrilling horse rides ended thereafter, when the horse trappers rode back to their reservation, yet told no one. Catching and taming horses were tasks usually handled by the men in the village, so it became quite a spectacle when the four youths rode in on two newly captured young stallions. Nearly everybody came out of their teepees once they heard the excitement, that 'Shadaiia, Nicco, Maharuk, and Coyote had returned with horses!' Both Walking Turtle and Shushuni, as well as the parents of Maharuk were extremely proud of their children's accomplishments. Even Chief Lakoatah who argued against the youngsters straying too far from their village, was extremely impressed.

CHAPTER
SIXTEEN

Despite constant scrutiny Miss Betty Lee remained a citizen of Jasper, in prime due to her financial assets and status, as the wealthiest unwed female in town. Unlike Mayor Rolley who relocated his family to another town, Betty Lee became the most desirable tramp in Jasper. Some of the town's prominent businessmen dated her, yet she refrained from committing herself to anyone. Many cowboys who spoke of her in a rather displeasing manner, during the scandal that cost Mayor Rolley his job, turned hypocrites in their desires to win her affections. Even though Betty Lee had an impressive list of important men from whom to choose, she idolized Mrs. Beth Becket, and wanted to become her. To achieve her goals, the ratchet gold digger engineered a plan to secretly seduce the mayor, knowing everything she did was being watched and scrutinized.

Betty Lee knew that the only place she could interact with Jonathan without spectators was at his office, therefore, she began visiting him over long periods of time, to minimize the gossip and avoid alerting Mrs. Becket. Mayor Becket had a small office next to the town's Registry Office, where they kept all the records of everything throughout Jasper's history. The Registry Office was run by Miss Rose-Mary Jingles, who was a renowned gossiper in town. After her first trip to the mayor's failed, Betty Lee went by the Registry Office and spoke with Rose-Mary about purchasing some property. When asked for what the land was to be used, Betty Lee indicated that she was considering opening a poultry ranch, thus, Rose-Mary suggested she spoke with the mayor?!

The first trip Betty Lee made to Jonathan's office was to congratulate him several weeks after his landslide victory. When the beautiful female reached the mayor's office, Jonathan was in a meeting with two of the town's business owners, therefore, she left. At her second visit months later, Betty Lee indicated to the secretary she was interested in opening her own poultry ranch, which she knew would spark a debate. Jonathan supported her poultry ranch idea and offered to mentor her to reach her goals. The mayor helped her to purchase a ten acers piece of land just outside of town, therefore, she did not have to endure the constant spies watching her in town.

The success driven female built a huge house on her property, fences it around, and built her chicken coop a slight distance away from the main building. To start her business, Betty Lee purchased six chickens and a rooster, but did everything by herself at first. After months away from town, Betty Lee unexpectedly showed up at Mayor Becket's office on a rainy day, wearing nothing but her nickers, beneath an ankle length leather jacket. After she entered the office and dropped her jacket, the mayor quickly locked the door, and indulged her sexual approach. For several years thereafter, no one else knew of their affair but his guards, thus, the mayor allowed Betty Lee to continue seeing the men who called on her.

The poultry business was slow in the beginning, but Betty Lee had to eventually hire a general helper and a maid. The male helper managed the hen house and collected the eggs, some of which they sold to customers. The maid she hired cleaned the house, sold the chickens and eggs, and handled the in-town chores. Even though a few women in town chose not to support her, Betty Lee's poultry business became a success. Regardless of her personal accolades, the opportunistic blond beauty was more than willing to prolong the adulterous affair, until she became Jonathan's wife.

Horace Becket

Following their liquor heist, Horace rode into town with Jim Pigston and left George and Dave Lexton to guard their stolen wagon. The bandits' intended to sell the entire shipment, then returned for the wagon after they got paid. With their plan arranged, they hid the stolen wagon a quarter mile out of town, among some trees and bushes. To avoid disrespecting his father, the first buyer Horace thought of was Jonathan, and thus went directly to see him once they arrived in Jasper.

Mute and Quick Draw were playing a card game inside the mayor's waiting room and, expected all guests to address them, for permission to enter their boss' office. Contrary to other visitors, Horace Becket had an impolite tendency of barging into his father office, without acknowledging anyone. Hence, he unexpectedly entered, walked directly pass both guards and entered the office without knocking.

"Horace, stop, don't go in th…" Quick Draw shouted, but was too late!

"Dad, I got a deal…" the young criminal was astonished to find Betty Lee bent over her father's desk, while they engaged in coitus!

"Wait son, this ain't what it seems like," Jonathan yelled, as he extracted himself and tried to fix his pants!

Horace slammed the door as he lowered his head and walked out of the office. The two guards whom he unexpectedly ran pass tried to express their sympathies, knowing that had they reacted much faster, they could have saved him the experience. Jim Pigston who waited outside by the front door, knew immediately that his friend had not struck a deal, after he spent less than a minute inside the establishment. Both men climbed onto their horses and rode down the street to J.T Pereau's place of business, where Horace surprisingly dismounted his horse and tied the animal to the stationary rail.

"Horace is you crazy, we can't let them know we the ones who stole their liquor," Jim warned!

"You coming or not," Horace demanded?

Jim was extremely nervous but had no choice but to follow Horace into the Showcase Lounge, which operated differently from Becket's Saloon. Instead of half naked women parading throughout the facility, the ladies inside the much classier establishment, wore elegant gowns, and were treated with respects by the customers. There was a female playing the piano and singing for those in attendance, while the hostess walked up and asked, 'if they wished to be seated?' Horace asked to speak with the owner Mr. Pereau, then got shown to a gentleman who was seated alone around a small table in a corner.

Contrary to Jonathan Becket, who always travelled with his guards, J.T. Pereau was a mild tempered individual, who did not care much for violence. Mr. Pereau had a love for the arts and would regularly travel across the country exhibiting his performers, but given the opportunities provided in Jasper, he decided to settle down. J.T had no children, his performers were his family members, and as a workaholic was married to his profession. There were limited resources in town to acquire the goods he needed to keep his establishment running, so it was quite possible to extort money from him.

"Are you Mr. Pereau," Jim asked, once they approached?

"What can I do for you gentlemen," J.T. Pereau enquired?

"If you want that liquor shipment of yours, it's gonna cost you double what you paid before," Horace exclaimed!

The mention of liquor shipment made Mr. Pereau rather uncomfortable, therefore, he discreetly offered both Jim and Horace a seat. Even though the business owner's table and chairs were positioned at a private section of the lounge, J.T still looked around to ensure there was no one close enough to hear their conversation.

"You the mayor's boy, ain't you," Mr. Pereau said?

"I'm my own man, and I ain't nobody's boy! Now either you pay up in the next five minutes or I take my business elsewhere," Horace threatened!

"You can't sell me what's mine, I already paid for that shipment," Mr. Pereau argued, before his anger gave way to reason! "Ok, ok! Wait here for a minute!"

J.T. left and went to a back room during which a waitress walked over and brought the bandits two glasses with liquor. Neither man had ever been inside the Showcase Lounge before, therefore, they enjoyed the performance while awaiting Mr. Pereau's return. As a precaution, Horace withdrew his Remington 38 and placed it on his lap underneath the table. After a few minutes, the own-er returned with a small bag, then sat back at the table.

"You playing a dangerous game kid," Mr. Pereau stated as he passed Horace the bag!

"Nice to see we reached an arrangement! Give us a short spell, and we be right back with your wagon," Horace exclaimed.

"No! You take me for a fool Becket? You go and bring back my wagon! Your friend stays right here until you get back," Mr. Pereau dictated!

Horace left with the payment and rode to the location, where they hid the wagon with their other accomplices. The moment Horace rode up, he tossed the sac of money to Dave, who quickly looked inside and grabbed a handful of currencies, as he cheered and celebrated. With Dave's attention focused on the money, Horace withdrew his firearm and shot him twice in the chest. Dave eyes opened wide with fright, as he fell backwards and scattered some of the money on the ground. George collected every dollar that fell and gave the sum to their young boss, who hid most of the money between some rocks for precautionary reasons. The two young cowboys then tied their horses to the back of the wagon and climbed into the box, where Horace handle the reigns as they rode back to town.

"I thought we was gonna split the money with Dave, why did you kill him," George enquired?

"He talks too much," Horace answered!

"Then why didn't you kill him round them liquor smugglers," George asked?

"Cause we can't have anyone finding those bodies and tying our operation together! Now can we," Horace reasoned?

"Yeah, I guess you is right," George noted!

Prior to arriving in Jasper, the bandits separated, wherein, George took another route into town. Horace awarded his partner enough time to get into position, before he brought the wagon into town, along the back road. The mayor's boy pulled up to the rear door of the Showcase Lounge, where he banged his fist against the door. George crept into position with his Winchester Rifle aimed at the exit, to assist his friends should anything unforeseen occurred. They knew there stood a chance that Mr. Pereau could arrange an ambush, but because he knew nothing of George, they maintained the element of surprise.

Horace went into the facility and re-emerged with J.T. Pereau, Jim, and two other gentlemen a few minutes later. Mr. Pereau had one of the men climb aboard the wagon and inspected the shipment, before Horace and Jim were permitted to leave. Immediately after the crooks left, the men began rushing to transport the liquor inside their facility.

CHAPTER
SEVENTEEN

As a young sixteen-year-old warrior Coyote was intellectually far beyond his years, and thus spent much of his leisure time in the company of the older men and women. For him to discover more about his roots and how his color toned people became members of the tribe, it was imperative that he listened to the stories of his elders. The young African Indian spent a lot of time learning from Kojoah, who was the oldest female in the village. Coyote learned that when his people were brought to America as slaves, several of them escaped once they got the chance. The escaped slaves tried to put as much distance between them and their slave masters, so they ran until they reached Cherokee territory. Many other slaves escaped, but some of them were killed when they trespassed on other savage Indian's land.

The Cherokee and the dark skinned African became blood brothers throughout the years, so there was never any animosity between them. Even though they were of the same tribe, there were certain differences between black Indians and their red skinned brother. Unlike the other warriors his age and older, who were more attracted to the slimmer Cherokee women, Coyote developed intimate feelings for Makayla, who was a full-bodied female.

There were instances where the young male warriors mischievously defied the rules to lust over the females. The main location from which they spied on the young maidens, was by the river while they bathed. Nicco and the rest of Coyote's village brothers would watch the slender Cherokee females bathing, but Coyote was the only person who focused on the larger sized females. The females never developed any sense they were being watched from the bushes, but Makayla and Shanayah would always bathe together.

One day the young African Indian observed Makayla and Shanayah leaving the village and followed them. The young ladies were heading out to pick some apples and grapes, which they used to make pastries. A short distance away the females sensed they were being followed, then noticed it was Coyote.

"Why do you follow us? We can take care of ourselves," Shanayah stated, before both females giggled to themselves!

"It is warrior's duty to keep women villagers safe," Coyote responded!

"You think you better than us," Shanayah quarrelled?

"Follow if you wish," Makayla responded!

Coyote walked directly behind both young ladies, who began whispering to each other. Makayla and Shanayah were older than Coyote by three years, so they were surprised his interest was not in the females his age. The fruit trees and vegetation were planted close to the village, so they did not have to walk far to gather the items. There were apples on the trees and grapes on the vines, which the three Indians began picking.

Shanayah went to pick a bunch of grapes, but was paying attention to Makayla, while she reached for the vines. There was a cobra snake resting beneath the vine, which Shanayah did not notice. As she brought her head around to focus on what she was doing, the snake leapt at her hand. Coyote was approximately ten feet away and observed the snake, as it sprang at the astonished female. To save the slow reactive female, the warrior withdrew his knife and threw it directly through the lunging snake.

Shanayah locked her eyes tight expecting to get bitten, but slowly reopened them to realize that the serpent had been killed. Her friend ran over to her and was ecstatic that she had not gotten bitten, due to Coyote's quick reflexes. The African descendant walked over, picked up the dead snake and removed his knife, before he stuffed the serpent inside their sac. Coyote nodded his head at both females, who were impressed by his warrior skills, thus, he nonchalantly returned to picking the fruits.

Later that evening Shanayah visited Coyote's family, with pastries she had made. Shushuni and Walking Turtle were elated to have her as a visitor and accepted the gift she brought. Nicco kept making fun of his brother for his taste in women, believing Coyote had interest in their visitor. Shanayah told everyone how Coyote saved her from the cobra, therefore, she felt compelled to thanking him. After another few minutes with the family, Shanayah took her leave, and got accompanied by Coyote. The young warrior behaved like a gentleman when he walked his visitor home, during which he questioned her about her friend.

"Again, my family thank you," Coyote stated!

"No, it is I who thank you! So, I honor your family," Shanayah responded!

They continued walking, but neither of them had much to say. Shanayah noticed that Coyote wanted to say something, but he was too nervous to speak his mind.

"Makayla likes you, you know," Shanayah declared?

"She does," Coyote questioned?

"She is nice to you, is she not," Shanayah countered?

"If that is your idea of nice, I guess," Coyote argued.

"Trust me, I see the way she looks at you! Makayla hardly laugh, yet she laughs at your dumb jokes. The same way you never smile, until I see you with her," Shanayah said.

"But I smile all the time," Coyote declared!

"Even now you speak of joy, yet there is no sign of happiness on your face," Shanayah indicated!

"I grow up not knowing my real mother and father! Walking Turtle has taught me everything he knows about my parents, and we honor them to this day! He has been a great replacement father, but I still, wish I met my true parents! So, I never had much to smile about," Coyote heartbrokenly related.

"I am sorry! I have heard the stories, but I did not know you feel like this," Shanayah responded.

"I never talk about this with anyone before," Coyote began.

"That's because you hardly talk to people," Shanayah joked!

Coyote smirked and said, "a wise warrior listens and learns, from everything that surrounds him!"

When they reached Shanayah's residence, she told him goodnight and went into her teepee. Coyote began walking back home, when he looked off into the distance and saw a coyote standing on a rocky ledge. The coyote was staring directly at him, before the animal looked up into the sky, and released a huge howl. The African Indian descendant had seen that coyote many times before, and felt it was the spirit of his ancestors, thus, he mimicked the animal's sound.

CHAPTER
EIGHTEEN

Mayor Becket rode up to his ranch house with Beth on their open back single horse wagon. Directly behind them were three of Jonathan's guards, who all headed for their quarters the moment the stable boy took a hold of the wagon's horse, to allow the Beckets to safely disembark.

"Good evening Mister and Misses Becket," greeted the stable boy!

"Evening Andy," Mrs. Becket responded!

"Is that my son's horse over by the barn," Jonathan asked?

"Yes sir," answered the stable boy!

"Is he inside the house," Jonathan demanded?

"Yes sir," said the stable boy!

"Did Jake and the boys returned from that cattle drive," Jonathan enquired?

"Not yet Mr. Becket," responded the stable boy!

It was another gruesome day for the couple, who seldom spent most their days in town attending to their individual affairs. Jonathan charged into the house and handed his maid his hat and gloves, as he walked pass her at the front door without acknowledging her.

"Good evening Mr. Becket! Evening to you ma'am," greeted the maid as the couple entered!

It was obvious that the mayor was deeply unset about something, as he went directly to his liquor cabinet and fixed himself a drink.

"Horace," Mayor Becket yelled!

"Please take it easy on him Jonathan," said Beth who walked into the room!

"How the hell do you expect me to take it easy as the mayor of Jasper? That boy stands to gain all of this and he chooses to waste it all!... Horace, get your butt down here this minute boy," Mayor Becket yelled!

Horace Becket came walking down the stairs from his bedroom, smoking a cigarette, and joined his parents inside the day's room. "Evening maw! What do you want paw?"

"Hello son," Beth responded!

"A criminal robbing businessmen? Ah, is that what you want to do with your life? I am the mayor for the people of Jasper, and I hear my son is stealing from these people," Mayor Becket exclaimed?

"Ain't no truth to them stories paw, people talk too much," Horace responded as he tried to dismiss the rumors!

"When was the last time you been to work? I gave you a job to stay out of trouble and gain some respect like a Becket," Mayor Becket argued!

"Like a Becket? Well, I'm tired of following in your footsteps, everybody these people always talking bout your daddy this, your daddy that, so you can keep your boring ass job and your mayor status, and I'll keep going on getting mine my way," Horace insisted!

"By swindling and robbing folks? Those people you taking from, may be crooked, and may not be that handy with a pistol, but they damn sure can hire people to pull that trigger," Mayor Becket exclaimed!

"Jonathan; Horace! Both of you stop that bickering right this minute! Y'all know how much I can't stand listening to people quarrel! I want both y'all to go wash up for supper, and we discuss all this later," Beth instructed!

"Ain't no criminal eating at my dinner table, or living under my roof," Mayor Becket declared!

"Jonathan stop that," Beth lamented!

"It's ok maw, I wasn't planning on sticking around here much longer anyways. It's obvious we don't see eye to eye, the good mayor ain't spent time with his only son in years! I guess the only person he got time for is that whore of his, Betty Lee," Horace disclosed!

"Huh," Beth surprisingly exclaimed at the disclosure!

"I pray you keep your name off the lawman's warrant list, because the day the sheriff mentions your name, I swear I'll give him the order to hunt you down and lock you away like the rest a them damn criminals," Mayor Becket warned!

"I ain't scared a no lawman daddy! And ain't no lawman gonna stop me from getting mine neither," Horace boasted!

"Get the hell out of my house and don't you come back until you change the way you live," Mayor Becket instructed!

"No Jonathan," Beth shouted!

"It's ok maw, I'll be fine! I'll check in on you from time to time," Horace stated as he tightly hugged his mother.

Young Becket ran up to his room and shoved some apparels inside his saddle bag, then strapped his gun belt around his waist. By the time Horace returned downstairs Beth was standing at the base of the stairs sobbing, while Jonathan remained inside the room smoking his cigar and drinking liquor. Beth embraced her son tightly and walked him to the front door, where she gave him a handful of currencies and advised him 'to be careful.' The moment Horace walked to his horse, then climbed aboard, Beth dried her tears, went into the kitchen, and selected a butcher knife from a drawer. With the knife at hand, Beth went back into the days room, where Jonathan was chugging his drink.

"How long have you been sleeping with that hoe," Beth demanded, as she moved toward Jonathan?

"That's all a lie! That boy was lying to you Beth," Mayor Becket declared, while moving away from his enraged wife!

After chasing her husband around some furniture, Beth stopped and threatened him, "I suggest you sleep in here for the next few nights! And pray to God I don't cut your throat while you sleep!"

Mrs. Becket stormed from the room thereafter and climbed the stairs to her bedroom. Jonathan was so nervous that he fixed himself another drink and swallowed it all in one gulp. The mayor then lit himself another cigar, and went outside onto the porch, where he smoked it. That night Mayor Becket stayed up all night watching the stairs, to see if his wife intended to carry out her threat. He dozed off around 5:08 AM and was awakened at 6:03 AM, by a firm slap across his jaw. Once Jonathan opened his eyes he froze, when he realized his wife held the knife to his throat.

"I gave you all night to think about it! Now, are you ever gonna mess with that hoe again," Mrs. Becket demanded?

"I swear honey! I will never touch her again," Jonathan begged!

"For your sake I pray you do not Jonathan, or Jasper is gonna need a new mayor," Beth stated!

CHAPTER
NINETEEN

akayla and Shanayah were walking to Shushuni's residence to surprise Coyote. As they walked along the back of the village, they came across a fist fight between Onacona and Tsiyi versus Coyote. There were three other teenage youths there, who were all cheering for Onacona and Tsiyi. When the females came along and tried rushing in to stop the fight, they were held and prevented by the spectators. While Onacona held Coyote's hands from behind, Tsiyi applied the beating with his bare fists. After several bone crushing blows to the body and face, Coyote's legs wobbled as if he was about to fall unconscious. Tsiyi thought he was about to land the pivotal knockout blow, therefore, he paused the battering to gloat.

"You shall forever be known as the orphan among us," warned Tsiyi, who then raised his fist to layout their opponent!

With Coyote falling forward, Onacona's hold on him began slipping. Everyone thought Coyote was already seeing twinkle stars, until he kicked Tsiyi directly in the groin. The aggressor grabbed for his crotch and tumbled to his knees directly in front of Coyote. The African Indian pulled his left hand free, stepped on Tsiyi's shoulder, and used his momentum to propel himself backwards over Onacona's head. While in midair Coyote twisted his body and landed facing the warrior who held him secure. Before Onacona could react, Coyote grabbed him around the waist, hoisted him over, and dropped him on the back of his neck.

Tsiyi mouth fell open with fright, but there was nothing he could do to stop the battleground dominator walking toward him. With such a devastating cramp affecting his ability to offer up a defense, Tsiyi held up his right hand to plea for forgiveness. When his comrades saw that Tsiyi was the one about to get knocked out, they released the females and rushed in to join the attack.

With both Onacona and Tsiyi rendered inoperative, Coyote began fighting off their three companions. From out of nowhere, Nicco came rushing in to help his brother, who was still holding his own regardless the challenge. The two brothers at that point made disposing of the bullies look rather easy, as they gave them a taste of their own medicine. After the brothers thoroughly thrashed the troublemakers, Tsiyi and Onacona gathered their associates and ran.

Coyote felt unappreciated by some of the things told to him during the conflict. The ratio of dark-skinned Indians to their tribal brother was 1 to 11, so he felt it was a necessity to increase their numbers. The African Indian's attackers had left him with several bruises and scars, so he felt embarrassed knowing the females saw him get dominated. To avoid the sympathetic gestures and shame, Coyote took off running to his horse. Makayla knew that he felt hurt and wanted to be alone, yet she took off running after him. Shanayah noticed that Nicco had gotten a bruised knuckle and had a tiny scar above his eyebrow.

"Oh, you are hurt! Let me help you," Shanayah insisted, as she took Nicco's hand into hers and used a cloth to wrap the bruise!

Nicco had never paid much attention to Shanayah until that instant, when he raised his eyes from the kind gesture being applied to his injured hand. The striking beauty of her hazel-colored eyes, and the warmth of her affections, made him reminisced on the pastries she brought his family. The young warrior recalled that, he never thanking her for the gesture, but would surely love to have some more of those pastries. There was an uncanny beauty that radiated from Shanayah, which Nicco had never before noticed. After watching the two brothers thrashed their five opponents, Shanayah felt enchanted by Nicco, but thought he preferred slimer females. To show his gratitude, Nicco placed his other hand atop Shanayah's, before he surrendered a pleasant smile.

Coyote ran to his white stallion, untied the animal, climbed aboard, and rode away. Makayla chased after Coyote until she reached the village's horse pen, where she borrowed someone's horse and went after him. The Africa Cherokee was trying to be alone, so he rode fast and hard to the waterfalls, a few miles away from their village. A few minutes after Coyote reached the waterfall and sat at his favorite spot, Makayla rode up and dismounted. The two of them had become good friends, but Coyote did not wish for anyone to see him in such a state. Even though the beautiful native Cherokee female, and the descendant of Africans, seldomly spent time together, they both cared deeply for each other.

"Coyote, are you OK?"

"Go back to village Makayla! I wish to be alone!"

Makayla ignored Coyote's instructions and went over and sat beside him, "Shanayah told me, how you feel about yourself. Even though your true mother and father, are among our ancestors, the villagers is still your family, and Shushuni and Walking Turtle, will always be your parents!"

"I know all this, but it's not the same!"

"We did not all come into this life with the same ability, but we must travel our path! My heart bleeds for your past loss, but you must not let this change your path!"

Makayla's powerful words brought tears to Coyote's eyes. Many of the youths from his village grew up without one of their parents, so Coyote believed in his heart he was not the only person who felt as such. The young warriors were taught to be fierce and tactful killers, so he never had any of his peers with whom he spoke. Walking Turtle was the only male who showed him affections about his lost parents, but it would have been more uplifting had he conversed with other village youths.

"Thank you," he calmly stated!

Makayla placed her left arm around his shoulder and hugged him gently. There was blood along the side of his face, which she used a cloth to wipe away, before she addressed the wound. The scenery was soothing as they sat quietly and looked off into the wild. While admiring the view, Coyote turned to look at Makayla and say something, but she was already staring at him, and thus kissed him. Having never passionately kissed someone before, Coyote was an amateur, but quickly became an expert. They both laid on the ground and appeased each other, until they made thrilling love for the first time.

CHAPTER TWENTY

One day Beth Becket went to see Dr. Frank Withers at his office, to acquire some pain medication. The Doc was alone at his practice and examined her, before he gave the patient a small bottle containing liquid medication, and instructions on how to take the drug. Dr. Withers gave Mrs. Becket a date on when to return and collected payment for the medicine. With their business concluded the doctor showed his patient to the door and welcomed in a waiting patient. As Beth exited through the front door she ran into Betty Lee, who was on her way in to see Dr. Withers, with a noticeable small bump at her stomach. The once courteous and polite female attempted to hide her belly and walked by without saying a word, however, Beth grabbed onto her arm and stopped her in her tracks. The personal guard who chauffeured Mrs. Becket started walking towards them from beside the wagon. Beth signalled him to stay back, therefore, he returned to his prior position.

"You may believe you got this whole town fooled, but I know you sleeping with my husband! Take this as your only warning, stay away from my husband," Beth threatened!

"If you could still please him, he would not come calling now would he, Mrs. Becket," Betty Lee answered?

"Listen I made you whatever it is you are in this town," Beth argued!

"And I suggest you never forget what it is that I know about your family," Betty Lee said!

"You're playing with the wrong woman little girl," Beth warned!

"It's only a matter a time, before I'm the one sleeping in your bed Mrs. Becket," Betty Lee advised as she tried to pull away her hand!

"There is just wide-open land out there for miles and miles, where nobody can find unmarked graves! I will have somebody bury you if necessary, so I suggest you do as told," Beth declared, before she released Betty Lee's hand altogether!

Following their altercation Betty Lee became fearful for her life, knowing the erroneous business practices of the woman she insulted. For protection Betty-Lee went to the sheriff's office and spoke with Sheriff Jeff McCall and Deputy Blank. During her disclosure she neglected to mention her past dealings with the Beckets, who was the most powerful couple in town. Sheriff McCall listened to the female's complaint, wherein she made herself seemed like the victim in an adulterous relationship.

While Deputy Blank thought about how they could assist the female, the sheriff tried to falsify her testimony and, made it seemed as if she was just being paranoid. The deputy was new to the territory, but from what he had learnt, the Beckets were accustomed to getting whatever they wanted. Deputy Blank also learnt from his counterpart, how the town's sheriff got elected to his post, and where his loyalty rested. Contrary to what Betty Lee said, Sheriff McCall argued that Mrs. Becket would never follow through with her threat, to ease Betty Lee's conscience. When Deputy Blank saw that the sheriff refused to provide any solution, he offered to ride out to her property occasionally, to check in on her.

Following the Becket's last argument, Beth began using her personal security detail, to get to and from town. When Beth Becket arrived home that evening, she advised Jonathan she was going for a ride, and went down to their stables. Beth left the house with a concealed weapon and planned to shoot Betty Lee. As she opened the door and walked into the stable, she saw one of the barn handlers urinating inside an empty stall.

"Hey! I told you boys no pissing in here! Go pack your shit and get off my ranch! You're fired," Beth stated!

"I am sorry Senora Becket! Please don't fire me," pled the Mexican helper?

Beth walked over to her horse's stall and called to the next barn handler. "Ramirez, saddle up my horse! I'm taking her out for a ride!"

The man who Beth fired walked up to her emotionally distort. "Please, Senora Becket I need this job? If I can do anything, please?"

Beth initially ignored the helper until a thought came to her, at which she reconsidered, then gave him an ultimatum. "If you want this job, and the chance to earn an additional two hundred dollars, there is one thing you can do! There is a woman who lives slightly out of town known as Betty Lee, who Mr. Becket impregnated. I want you to visit her and strangle the life from her body!"

The demand made of the Mexican was criminal in nature, but jobs were scarce, and he could not afford to lose his position. "Si Senora Becket, I do this thing for you!"

Instead of riding to Betty Lee's house as planned, Beth went for a pleasant ride along the plains, during which she felt confident she would be rid of her husband's lover. That same night Louis accompanied his co-worker Ramirez to Betty Lee's farm, where he agreed to serve as a lookout while his workmate did what Mrs. Becket requested. Both barn handlers stationed their horses off the property a short distance away and went the rest of the trail on foot. When they reached the house, Betty Lee was inside her bedroom laying on her bed reading a book, after not being able to fall asleep due to nervous tensions.

Ramirez broke a small pane of glass built into the door, then reached in for the lock, and opened the back door. Betty Lee heard when the glass broke and quickly blew out the lantern by her bed, while she retrieved her handgun from her night table. As she attentively listened to decipher who was inside her house, she aimed her 36 mm revolver towards the door and held it steady. With Louis camped outside in the shadows looking out, Ramirez crept into the house and went directly to Betty Lee's bedroom. The home invaders thought the female was asleep at that hour, and assumed she was unarmed. As the intruder appeared in the doorframe, Betty Lee fired two bullets and shot him in the left shoulder and arm, at which he staggered backward and without hesitation ran from the house.

When the Mexicans returned to the ranch, Louis brought Ramirez to the maid's quarters, where the female helper extracted the bullet, and cleaned the wound. Beth Becket was awaiting the result of the invasion and entered during the process, at which she was made aware of what happened. With Betty Lee still breathing, Beth knew that she could easily be found guilty of accessory to commit murder, should the law search her property and found the injured intruder. As a result, she went to Jonathan's office, took two thousand dollars from his money drawer, and gave it all to Ramirez to flee the country. Once the injured worker was patched up, Beth had the maid prepared food for his voyage, and promised him his job would be secure when he returned. Mrs. Becket also instructed Ramirez to contact Louis regularly by letter, and never mention any of what he had done. Louis was given a sturdy horse for his trip to Mexico and left the compound before daybreak.

Early the next morning Sheriff McCall visited the victim's ranch, where his deputies were on scene with Betty Lee. Following the victim's testimony, he looked over the evidence at the rear door and spoke with his detectives about what happened. The scared homeowner wanted the lawmen to search the Becket's ranch for the man who broke into her home. Betty Lee was convinced the intruder would be found there, but Sheriff McCall was not at all convinced. When asked 'if she had any idea who else would want to kill her,' instead of laying blame Betty Lee simply rubbed her stomach and thought of her evolving opportunities.

When Betty Lee realized Sheriff McCall would not further the investigation, she thought of her unborn child and took the next morning's stagecoach back to San Diego. In fear of their lives, Betty Lee took an extended trip and spent the next thirteen months with her mother Catherine. When Betty Lee left Jasper only a few people knew of her condition, but most importantly Beth Becket believed she had moved away for good. Throughout the course of her stay with her mother, Betty Lee mentioned nothing of her unborn child's father, but illustrated she could manage alone through her spending. A few days before her seventh month in San Diego, Betty Lee went into labour and gave birth to a healthy baby boy, whom she named Adam Lee Becket.

CHAPTER TWENTY-ONE

Coyote's life changed completely two months after he first made love to Makayla. The African Cherokee finished eating supper with his family one evening, and was conversing among themselves, when Makayla and her parents visited. Makayla's father Kanuna called out to Walking Turtle, who stood up and went out to greet him. When Walking Turtle exited, Makayla had her head lowered as if something terrible had happened.

"Hello, my friend, welcome," Walking Turtle greeted!

"We come to discuss Makayla with you," Kanuna declared!

"Come in, enter, do come in," Walking Turtle invited!

As soon as he re-entered his teepee, Walking Turtle asked his other children to leave, except Coyote who was the topic of discussion. Makayla kept her head pointed to the ground and refused to look up at anyone, which led Coyote to develop a nervous feeling. The young warrior had never felt so petrified through all the dangers he had faced, but he had confidence that whatever the issue his parents would help him mend it.

"Tell us, what is wrong," Shushuni asked?

"It is Makayla, we believe she carries a child," said Makayla's mother!

"Are you sure of this," Shushuni asked?

"It has been two months since she last bleed," the mother said.

"This is exciting news, is it not," Shushuni stated, as her face lit up like a Christmas tree?

The excitement tone in Shushuni's voice gave Makayla an enlightenment, knowing she would not be shunned for getting pregnant before marriage. The expecting mother slowly raised her head and made eye contact with Coyote, before she noted the pleasant smiles on Walking Turtle and Shushuni's faces. Coyote went from concern to jubilation, having felt the pressure to produce children to prolong his race.

Over the next few months, Makayla and Coyote prepared to welcome their first child into the world. While most people were genuinely happy for the couple, Nicco refuted the arrangement, with the belief that he was losing his brother. The two families began operating as one, to arrange whatever their siblings needed to manage a home. Nicco, Walking Turtle, Kanuna, and Coyote gathered several days after the arrangement, and went out into the bushes to get supplies to build a teepee. When they returned home with the branches they chopped from several trees, they aligned them and tied them together, then dug holes, and secured them into the ground. With the base for the teepee structured, the Indians used a huge, dried animal skin covering, stitched together by their women, and encased the dwelling.

Their village population had increased drastically due to the number of children conceived over the years. Chief Lakoatah was always encouraged by the birth of more children in the village, therefore, he was ecstatic to hear of the young lovers' addition. Kanuna and his wife did not wish for their daughter to be classified as an unwed tramp, so they emphasized to Shushuni the importance of Coyote marrying Makayla, before the birth of their child. To appease Makayla's parents, Coyote made arrangement for Chief Lakoatah to marry them, four months into their pregnancy. The young parents became the first in many Cherokee categories, considering they were the youngest couple ever tied by the chief, and they were the first couple wedded since their humongous ceremony.

Nicco thought that he would have lost his brother once Coyote committed himself to his new family, but he could not have been any further from the truth. The two brothers hunted and fished more together, than when Coyote resided with his parents. They spent so much more time together that his relationship with Shanayah grew, because they saw each other quite often.

It was customary for the entire village to attend important ceremonies such as weddings and funerals, so everyone went to Makayla and Coyote's affair. Even though Coyote was born into the tribe, he never felt more pride than being joined to a female from the village. The young lovers had a fabulous ceremony, where they got celebrated by the villagers who wished them long life and prosperity.

Following Chief Lakoatah's ceremony, the couple sat down to enjoy the dance performances. Coyote was barely old enough to drink and smoke, yet Walking Turtle treated him like an equal and offered them to him. As the couple sat watching, Tsiyi, Onacona, and the other three youths they fought with walked up.

"I give to you my respect Coyote! I also apologize to your woman, for calling her a fat swine," Tsiyi declared!

Coyote had not mentioned anything about the reason for the fight to Makayla, therefore, he tried signalling Tsiyi to stop talking by tapping his lips with his index finger. Onacona and the other three young warriors agreed with Tsiyi, so they shook their heads agreeably.

"We accept your apologies," Coyote stated!

Makayla had no idea Coyote was fighting over her honor that dreadful day. The female looked over at her new husband and felt pride having married him. Coyote's sisters and Makayla's siblings danced up a storm to show their happiness with the marriage. Even though Coyote exhumed a pleasant smile, Makayla knew that his heart wished his parents were there, so she leaned over to him and said, "I know your parents are watching over you this day!" The words spoke truth to what Coyote was feeling; therefore, a single tear ran from his right eye.

CHAPTER
TWENTY-TWO

Lance Callahan was a banker turned prospector who moved to Jasper in search of gold. The middle-aged man thought he would find fortune, then return east to enjoy the rest of his days. Lance worked as a banker for nearly thirty years, until an old man walked into his bank to deposit his retirement funds; and told him a story about gold. The old man's story was so believable that Lance quit his job that same day, went home and packed his belongings, then brought his wife and son across the country to Jasper. After several years of searching without any major discovery, Lance decided to return east as a pauper, where his family would assist him.

To get some food and travelling supplies, Lance went into town the evening before his scheduled departure, to exchange his prospecting equipment at the hardware store. The angry gold miner rode his single horse wagon, which was their transportation means to get back east. Following the equipment exchange, disappointment and embarrassment led the prospector into Becket's Saloon, where he planned on having one drink. The first shot of whiskey led to the second, before guilt convinced him to drown his sorrows in alcohol. The more liquor Lance swallowed, the more talkative and demonstrative he became of Mayor Becket.

The venue was nearly full, with most of the regulars who had witnessed many atrocities throughout the years. There were several drinkers at the bar beside Lance, who all began slowly moving away from beside him, once he persisted with badmouthing the mayor. Even the waiter tried advising the disappointed prospector, to refrain from disgracing Mayor Becket, nevertheless, he carried on with his rant.

"I can't wait till I get back east! When I get back east, one of the first things I'm gonna do, is place an ad in the papers, to let everybody, know about this here, gold scam in Jasper! You people act like, you don't know, what I'm talking about, but y'all know, Mayor Becket, behind everything that goes on, round here," Lance lamented!

"Mister, it might be best you stop drinking right now! And, for your own good, I suggest you stop talking bout the mayor as such," the waiter stated!

"Ain't nobody scared of your cheating ass mayor! Someone ought to, put a bullet between his eyes! If I ain't had to head back east, I would do it myself," Lance shouted as he staggered to stand aloft.

Sheriff McCall walked into the saloon and caught the last part of Lance's statement. The sheriff could tell the customer was drunk, by the manner with which he staggered about. Jeff walked up behind the prospector, who was facing the bar and demanding another drink. As the sheriff drew closer, Lance saw him approaching through the mirror behind the liquor bottles on the shelf. Fearing it might have been one of the mayor's guards, Lance withdrew his Colt 38mm sidearm and pointed at Sheriff McCall.

"Oh, it's you sheriff," Lance declared, before he started lowering his weapon!

Sheriff Jeff McCall felt embarrassed by the prospector, therefore, he withdrew his revolver and shot the man in the chest. Everybody inside the saloon were surprised when they heard a weapon discharged, believing that the gold digger had shot their sheriff. Lance grabbed for the wounded area and slowly crumbled to the ground, while Sheriff McCall re-holstered his weapon.

Early the next morning Lance's wife walked into town with their young son. Her husband had not returned, and they were supposed to hit the trail early, so the wife got concerned and headed into town. When they reached Jasper, the wife headed directly to the jail, expecting to either find her husband there, or get some information on his whereabouts. Deputy Blank had recently gone on duty and did not know about the incident that took place the prior evening. Sheriff McCall had gone home for a few hours, yet was scheduled to return to the office some time that morning. Deputy Marks was at home until later that evening, when he was scheduled to work.

Mrs. Callahan saw their single horse wagon outside the hardware store, where she entered and asked, 'if they had seen her husband?' The servers at the hardware store stated that 'they saw Lance the evening prior, but had no idea where he might have gone.' When they went to the jailhouse and Deputy Blank told them 'he did not know where Mr. Callahan was,' they had no idea where else to look at that point.

Gus noticed that the woman and her son were tired after doing all that walking, so he offered to find her husband while they rested at the jail. The deputy went to Becket's Saloon first, where he expected to get some information about the man's whereabouts. The saloon was empty at that hour of the morning, and the only person available was the establishment cleaner. While cleaning the floor, the worker mumbled to himself continuously like a psychotic individual.

"Ain't no more law in Jasper, this old town ain't what it used to be. People getting killed, nobody seem to care..." the cleaner mumbled to himself as he moped!

Deputy Blank walked into the saloon and noticed that the cleaner was moping blood from the floor by the bar.

"Did somebody get shot last night," Deputy Blank asked?

"Yes sir, deputy! Sheriff McCall shot that gold digger who was trash talking the mayor," the cleaner said after he realized who it was!

"I saw the sheriff earlier, but he ain't said nothing bout no shooting," Deputy Blank stated.

"More like a slaughter if you asked me," the cleaner said under his breath!

"What did you just say," Deputy Blank demanded?

"Listen deputy, I don't want no trouble, but it's getting to where you can't talk bout certain folks round these parts! That man got a little liquored up, and was mouthing off bout the mayor, but he ain't deserved to get shot down like that by the sheriff," the cleaner declared!

Deputy Blank left the saloon and went to the doctor's office, where Lance's body was resting in a Pine Box. Inspection of the body revealed the single gunshot wound to the chest, which killed the prospector instantly. As he headed back to the jailhouse, the deputy pondered why the sheriff neglected to mention the shooting. The man's family was awaiting news about him and Deputy Blank had no justifiable cause why he was killed. When he reached the jail, it took the deputy a few seconds before he opened the door and entered.

"Oh deputy, please tell us you found my husband," the wife asked?

"I'm sorry Mrs. Callahan, but I have terrible news about your husband," Deputy Blank began.

Mrs. Callahan sensed there was something wrong and grabbed her son immediately. They both began weeping and cuddled together, as Gus continued.

"I'm afraid he was shot and killed last night," Deputy Blank stated.

"I don't see anybody in these cells! So, where is the man who killed my husband," Mrs. Callahan demanded?

"From what I found out, it seems like Sheriff McCall shot him," Deputy Blank answered!

Mrs. Callahan's face became hardened, as she wiped away the tears from her eyes. The female stood up and firmly held onto her son's hand, before she angrily walked to the front door, and opened it. Sheriff McCall was about to enter the jailhouse, when the door flew open with Mrs. Callahan and her son.

"You murderer! You shot and killed my husband, but your day will come! Mark my words sheriff, your day will come," Mrs. Callahan threatened, before she spat at the lawman's feet, and walked by!

"You have a fine day Mrs. Callahan," Sheriff McCall exclaimed!

CHAPTER
TWENTY-THREE

To acquire certain essential products such as rifles and ammunition, which were manufactured by Caucasian companies, the Cherokee Indians made an arrangement with Jikaranchi. The Cherokee tribe was banned from acquiring new weaponry by the president, who still used legislations to punish them for the uprising. Because of Jikaranchi's half Caucasian background, he was exempted from the law, therefore, Chief Lakoatah gave him their Buffalo, Moose, and Deer Skins, which he in turn traded at Becket's Hardware Store. The Indians also gave their secret trader some gold nuggets and precious stones to acquire the goods the needed. To avoid raising any suspicions, Jikaranchi was advised to make multiple trips to the hardware store. As a result, the trader made two separate trips over a three-week span, where he brought portions of their merchandise to exchange. The first trip went through without any issues, wherein Jikaranchi traded his products and received eight Winchester rifles and two boxes of bullets.

Three and a half weeks later the Indian trader returned to the hardware store, with another pile of fur skin and gems to trade. The products were again exchanged for ten Winchester Rifles, bullets, and other supplies, before Jikaranchi tied his purchases onto a mule, then began the journey back to his cottage. The Indian's loyal dog Savage was always with him and kept his company wherever he went. Immediately after Jikaranchi left, the young helper Robin from the hardware store ran down to the motel, and knocked on apartment five, where Horace was sleeping in bed with a whore.

"Who the hell is it," Horace demanded?

"It's Robin from the hardware store," whispered the salesboy!

Horace climbed out of bed butt naked, with his hand pistol at hand, and slightly opened the door.

"What is it?"

"That half Indian hermit who lives out there in the wilderness, just traded another stack of fur and some other stuff for rifles and two boxes of ammunition," Robin whispered!

"Where was he heading," Horace questioned?

"He was heading south, with the guns packed on that lazy mule of his," Robin whispered, before he looked around to see if anyone saw him, then left!

Horace closed the door and walked back over to the bed, where he sat the edge, poured himself a drink from a bottle, and chugged it down. While getting dressed his lady friend rolled over and noticed him getting ready to leave.

"Where you going so early, it's barely pass midday," asked the whore?

"I got business to take care of girl," Horace stated!

"Will I see you later tonight," questioned the female as she picked up a cigarette and lit it?

"Can't rightly say, but you'll be the first to know," Horace declared.

Young Becket took some money from his pocket and left the dollars on the night table before he exited. The bandit leader knocked doors to apartment three and two as he passed by and shouted, "we leave in five minutes boys!" Within two minutes George and Jim exited their motel doors, where they both left the whores they spent the night with. The three bandits allowed Jikaranchi to put some distance between them, before they rode out of town and unknowingly followed him back to his residence.

When Jikaranchi arrived at home he unpacked the items he bought and brought them into his cottage. Moments later Horace and his associates arrived on the scene and dismounted off their horses in the bushes. The band of crooks scoped out the cottage to ensure the area was clear, before they moved in. Savage smelt the group of bandits and started barking to alert his owner, who looked through a window to see if anyone was in his yard. Jikaranchi grabbed for his rifle and stood by the front door with Savage, who ran out into

110

the yard and continued barking.

"Nicco, Coyote, is that you out there," Jikaranchi yelled speaking Cherokee, but nobody answered?

Savage began barking intensely and ran to three different area around the cottage, as if whoever was hiding in the woods had separated and were getting closer. Jikaranchi summoned Savage to his side and the dog returned but continued barking irritably.

"My dog is not the only one that can smell you White Man! Come out of the bushes, or I send in the dog," Jikaranchi sighted!

Horace walked out into the open but stood closer to the wooded area. Jikaranchi quickly aimed his weapon at him, while his dog continued barking at the other bandits.

"What do you want on my land," the half Indian demanded?

"I was told that you went into the town this morning and bought yourself a few rifles! Now what they forgot to tell you back in Jasper, was that you gotta pay taxes on them there guns, so I'm gonna have to confiscate all a them firearms," Horace exclaimed!

"I suggest you turn around and get off my property before I kill you where you stand," Jikaranchi threatened!

"Chick-chick, chick-chick," sounded two weapons at different areas across the treeline!

"Woof-woof," Savage continuously barked!

"If you want to live, I suggest you put down that there weapon of yours! Or my friends gonna kill you, plus your dog, and then we go take them guns," Horace warned!

"Quiet Savage," shouted Jikaranchi as he slowly lowered his rifle and dropped it on the ground!

"Now, where are those guns we were talking about," Horace asked?

"Those guns do not belong to you or me," Jikaranchi argued.

"I don't care who those weapons belonged to! They ours now, so kindly show Jimbo here where you got them hid, and we'll be on our merry way! George, get his horse so we can use it for transport," Horace instructed!

"Grrrrr," growled the wolf dog at the bandits!

"Bam," sounded Jim's weapon as he shot Savage!

Jikaranchi's eyes widened with fright as he stared down at his injured pet, then dropped to both knees. Tears immediately began rolling down the half Indian's face as he scooped up the bleeding wolf dog's head into his hands, and rested his face against the animal's.

"Why the hell did you have to shoot the damn dog," George declared?

"I didn't like the way that animal was staring at me! Hey, you heard my friend, get up and bring us to those guns before the same thing happens to you," Jim stated, as he walked up and kicked Jikaranchi away from his dying pet!

Jim moved in to kick Jikaranchi again, when an arrow shot from in the woods struck him directly in the chest. The shock from being shot stopped Jim from following through with his devious intent, whereby he dropped to the ground and held onto the arrow. Horace quickly dropped to one knee and began intently looking in the woods, as he aimed his rifle directly at Jikaranchi.

"Whoever you are out there, one more arrow and your friend is the next to die out here," Horace threatened!

George who was retrieving Jikaranchi's horse to stack the weapons onto, dived onto the ground to make himself a harder target. Following Horace's warning no other arrows were fired, before a calm sat over the property. Jikaranchi crawled back to his dying pet, lifted the animal onto his lap, and hugged it gently as it passed away.

"That there is an Indian arrow stuck in Jim's chest! Maybe the guns belong to them," George frightfully stated?

"Shut up and keep your head down you idiot! I'll handle this," Horace stated! "Now, I'll have whoever you are know that my name is Horace Becket, and my father is the mayor of the town of Jasper! So, if anything happens to me there will be trouble for your people!"

"That's right Horace, tell them to step outta them bushes," George whispered!

"Whoever y'all are, I want you step outta them bushes right now, or I'll shoot your friend over here," Horace shouted!

A deafening silence fell across the property, which made the cowboys fearsome, not knowing what the warriors in the woods intended. There was a group of five Cherokee warriors among the shadows underneath the trees watching. The group included Onacona, Maharuk, Nicco, Laquary and Coyote. Nicco and his brother signalled their associates to remain hidden, while they prepared to face the Caucasian tyrants. Contrary to their comrades' beliefs, Nicco and Coyote stepped from the shadows seconds later, and stopped by the edge of the woods.

"Holy shit, that's a colored Indian! I've heard bout them from paw, but I ain't never seen none a them in person," Horace whispered to George!

"Jonathan Becket? Is that the man you speak of as your father," Coyote asked?

"Yeah, that's my paw! What is it to you Indian," Horace bragged?

Coyote withdrew his knife, took two steps from Nicco, and pointed the blade at Horace.

"Your father is son of a whore, who killed our fathers, so I challenge you to a fight! If you win, you and your friend may go free," Coyote declared!

"No colored Indian is gonna call my grand-nanny a whore! I accept your challenge Indian! It's about time someone taught you to respect my kind," Horace stated!

Coyote passed Nicco the rest of his apparels and walked towards Horace with his knife at hand. Horace unbuckled his gun belt and passed it to George, then withdrew a knife from his boots.

"Cut him up mighty fine Horace," George cheered!

Both Coyote and Horace circled each other, as they stared into each other's eyes with their knives ready to puncture. They both made several faints and swiped at each other, yet they were more cautious in the beginning. The cowboy stabbed at his opponent several times, before he made the pivotal mistake, that allowed the Indian to grab a hold of his outstretched wrist. The Cherokee warrior spun his opponent into a choke hold, at which Horace dropped his knife and grabbed onto Coyote's hand. Horace and Coyote tussled in the dirt, as the cowboy attempted to prevent being stabbed.

Horace was deceptively strong and held Coyote from inserting his blade. The African Cherokee struggled to insert his knife, until he snatched his hand from around Horace's neck, and clawed his fingernails across his eyes. The cowboy's grip weakened when he reached for his injured eyes with his opposite hand. Coyote seized the opportunity and plunged his knife into the throat of the man, whose father murdered his father.

Nicco released a loud warrior's chant, to illustrate his approval of the killing. George's mouth dropped wide open with disbelief, as Coyote pushed his friend's dead body aside, and rose to his feet. Coyote proceeded to kneel on Horace's back, then used his knife to scalp the cowboy, while his friend watched nervously.

"Yeh-yeh-yeh-yeh…" Coyote shouted after he removed a large patch of Horace's scalp!

The other three Cherokee warriors stepped from the shadows and startled George, who threw both his hands high into the air. George thought they would have killed him to prevent word circling about Horace Becket, but the Cherokee Indians were trustworthy people, who stood by whatever they said.

"You may go free," Coyote exclaimed!

George went and retrieved their horses, then threw Horace's body onto his saddle, and rode away with the body. Nicco and the other Indians went to Jikaranchi and offered their sympathies for the loss of his beloved pet, knowing what the animal meant to him. Once Coyote cleaned himself up and joined his friends, Jikaranchi told them what he felt Horace's killing might mean.

"The father to the man you just killed, will stop at nothing until he has gained his revenge! This man, Jonathan Becket, was responsible for your people nearly being extinct, many moons ago! People say it was his dream to wipe out the Cherokee; but I am certain, given a second chance he will not fail this time! The Nevada Cherokee has only one option to survive; they must flee from this land, and move to Mexico," Jikaranchi stated!

"That is no option, Chief Lakoatah will never agree to this! The Cherokee will never leave, Cherokee land," Onacona declared!

"Until we learn otherwise, Lacquary, go to Jasper Town, and report home if anything change! We shall bring this matter before the council, and have them decide," Nicco instructed!

The Indians collected the supplies their friend acquired for them and brought them along. The young warriors wanted Jikaranchi to accompany them to their village, but he declined and insisted 'he must first bury his dog!' Despite their predicament, Jikaranchi was extremely happy his young friend had avenged his father. The hurt from losing one's only son, would scald the father's memories forever, so Coyote and Nicco felt proud having killed Mayor Becket's offspring. Lacquary rode to Jasper to serve as their eyes and ears, in case the cowboys decided to attack their village.

CHAPTER
TWENTY-FOUR

L acquary rode to Jasper, where he dismounted his horse a quarter mile from town. The Cherokee Indian removed the blanket he sat on from the horse's back, then slapped the animal on the rear. The stallion took off running back to their village, which was customary for their trained animals. The warrior threw the blanket over his head and slowly walked into Jasper, where the citizens looked at him with disgust. Some of the citizens were impartial towards Indians, while others mistreated and shunned them.

Lacquary pretended he was a pauper begging for money and sat on the sidewalk across the road from Becket's Saloon. The Indian kept his head covered with the blanket, as he lifted his open palm to residents who went by. Some of the locals donated to the Indian's cause, but most of them passed by and ignored him. The first few hours in Jasper were relatively quiet, but Lacquary expected some sort of uprising, once news broke of Horace's killing. He thought that George would have ridden directly into town, so he strolled down to the Mayor's Office, which was closed.

Lacquary began getting concerned, after several hours passed without any sighting of George. He walked to the Sheriff Office and lingered outside along the sidewalk, where he could clearly hear the lawmen inside. The two deputies left the jailhouse minutes later and went on a surveillance tour of the town. After the deputies walked pass Lacquary, he allowed a few minutes to pass, before he changed location, and returned to his first post. Whenever the business owner whose store he sat in front of, chased him away, Lacquary relocated to either the Jailhouse or the Mayor's Office.

*

George wasted no time and rode directly to Mayor Becket's ranch. Jonathan and Beth were seated out on their verandah, drinking wine, and enjoying the beautiful evening, when George rode up to the house. Despite his personal grievances with his son, Jonathan ran out into the yard and met George, as he rode to a stop. Beth slowly walked towards the corpse with disbelief, before she fell to both knees, and wept in the dirt.

Mrs. Becket took the news rather difficult and immediately began blaming her husband for Horace's death. Jonathan made George explained everything that happened, but instead of admitting they were involved in a weapons heist, the young man lied. George told Jonathan that they were only looking to have a little fun, when they visited Jikaranchi's cottage. After listening to George's account of the incident, Beth went to retire and mourned inside her house. Before she walked away, the grief-stricken mother commanded Jonathan, 'to hang whosoever committed the injustice against their son!'

While Horace's body got transported inside, where his mother and the maid cleaned him up and dressed him, Jonathan summoned several of his gunners. Mayor Becket stood on his verandah and addressed Quick Draw and six of his gunners, who were all mounted in their horses' saddles. The mayor had begun drinking heavily and held a bottle of Whiskey at hand, while some of the guards loaded bullets into their weapons. Night had fallen across the territories and everyone on the ranch was terribly depressed by Horace's killing. Beth Becket demanded that blood be spilt, but Jonathan understood the ramifications of acing hastily, so he conjured a plan that would benefit them eventually.

"You boys bring along them Indian apparels," Jonathan asked?

"We sure did boss," Quick Draw answered, at which Jonathan took a drink from his bottle!

"Until the light a day, I want y'all to ride about them outskirts and raise more hell than them Cherokee did years back! I want every house that y'all come across burnt to the ground, kill every man, woman, and child, and make sure you don't leave no witnesses! Then pay that half Indian who ambushed my boy a special visit! Gentlemen make sure all this look like them savage Indians done it! Am I understood," Jonathan ordered?

"Yes sir, boss," exclaimed the gang of cowboy assassins before they rode off into the night!

Quick Draw and the six marauders headed north and reached their first arson location twenty minutes later. The cabin they came across was relatively small with a single bedroom attached, that was owned by a middle-aged couple, who relocated there two years prior. Sue and Henry Russel were relaxing in bed, after a long day toiling over their chores, but had no idea they were being targeted by the group. When Quick Draw and his blood thirsty associates reached the cabin, he instructed them to surround the residence, while he remained hidden in the woods. The mayor's main gun-hand covered the front entrance should anyone had attempted to escape.

Jonathan's gunners got into position, then whistled to inform Quick Draw they were in place. Henry Russel heard the alerting whistles, so he sat up in bed and listened more attentively. With everyone in place, three of the gunners unwrapped bow and arrows, which they hid during transport. All three men armed their bows with modified arrows, then set the arrows ablaze, and fired them at the cabin. The murderers waited and watched as the residence slowly burned, until the building was fully engulfed.

Sue was comfortably relaxing when she first smelt smoke. Henry was already sitting up in bed listening, but heard nothing further to prolong his concerns.

"You smell something burning Henry?"

Henry did not wish to worry his wife, therefore, he neglected to mention his concerns. Sue sniffed the air inside their room until she got out of bed and looked through the window.

"Henry, the house is on fire," Sue shouted!

"Let's get out of here Sue, I'll go try and put it out," Henry stated!

"I need to grab a few things first," Sue responded!

Henry jumped up and saw the flames through the window, so he ran out of the bedroom in his body length Long Johns, to fight the fire. The instant Henry opened the front door, and stepped into view, Quick Draw shot him with his Winchester Rifle. The Caucasian male dropped between the door frame where he laid motionless. Sue ran to her husband's aide and knelt beside his body, as she wept and shook his body for him to wake. Quick Draw took aim at Sue Russel and shot her also, thus, she tumbled onto her deceased husband. The arsonists all watched the cabin burn to ensured there was no one left alive, before they gradually moved on to their next stop.

An adequate number of settlers moved into the region following the Cherokee uprising, nearly twenty years prior. Most of the homes were scattered far apart and so it took some time for Becket's boys to reach their next target. The second cabin they came across belonged to a family of five, that included mother Hazel, father Nathan, and their four children Isiah, Moses, Luke, and Sarah. All the children were two years apart in age beginning with Isiah who

117

was their eldest at fifteen. Both parents were God fearing people and named the children after some of their favorite bible characters.

Hazel was a former schoolteacher, so she home taught the kids their academic lessons. Nathan's father was a preacher, so he provided the family ministry and discipline. The family grew most of their food on their land, hunted, fished, and set traps to catch rodents such as wild rabbits.

When Becket's group of arsonists reached the cabin it was quite late, yet there were shadows and a lamp burning through the main room's window. The band of marauders approached with the same attack strategy, wherein they surrounded the residence, then fired enflamed arrows at the structure. Hazel was feeding Sarah a teaspoon of medicine when they observed the flames building on the outer walls of the cabin. The concerned mother instructed Sarah to go wake her father, while she raced outside to attend to the fire, before it reached an uncontrollable level. On her way into her parents' bedroom, Sarah overheard a rifle shot and turned back to check on her mother. As she approached the front door, Nathan who had also heard the shot and came out to investigate, grabbed, and pulled her back inside. The young girl was fortunate, when a milli-second later a second bullet bored into the wooden door.

"Hazel, is you alright," Nathan shouted, but received no response, so he slammed the door?

"But daddy mommy is outside," Sarah cried!

"I know honey, but there are some bad people out there also," Nathan explained!

By then Isiah, Luke, and Moses had awoken and came out into the days' room to enquire what was happening. The smoke and heat from the fire had begun to affect Nathan and his children, therefore, they needed to find a way to exit the burning structure.

"I don't know who you are, but I got four children who is fitting to burn to death in here, unless they get out safely! Please, do I have your word you won't hurt my children," Nathan shouted, but again no response?

Sarah began coughing and crying loudly, while the others tried to cover their mouths and nostrils. As the dangers quickly escalated, Nathan found himself at an impasse, where they either stayed inside and died, or vacate the cabin. The God-fearing father held his children behind him, and opened the door to escape the developing furnace, when Quick Draw shot him in the upper right shoulder. The force of the bullet pitched him to the ground, therefore, he used his foot and kicked the door closed. All four children attended to their father, as he laid on the floor wounded and unable to save them. The children held tightly onto each other's hands and eventually succumbed to smoke inhalation, before they all burnt to death in the fire.

The gang of arsonists would destroy two other residences that night, before they went to Jikaranchi's cottage to torcher him for his involvement in Horace's killing. Their final location early that morning was the only appointment at which they attacked with a different strategy. Instead of surrounding the cottage, Quick Draw sent two men to the rear of the structure, to watch the back window should Jikaranchi try to flee, while he and the others went directly to the front door. With their weapons drawn and at the ready, Quick Draw and his followers kicked in the front door, then barged into the cottage to find Jikaranchi unconscious in bed. The Indian had gotten intoxicated after he buried his faithful dog, before he later passed out with the bottle in hand. Two of the cowboys snatched Jikaranchi from his bed and dragged him outside onto the lawn, where they stumped and beat him to within a faction of his life.

Mute climbed onto his horse, after they tied a rope around Jikaranchi's neck, and threw the opposite end of the rope over a nearby tree branch. With his companions cheering and crying for blood, Mute wrapped the rope around the horn on his saddle, then slapped his horse for the animal to gallop. The battered and beaten anatomy of the Half Indian got strung up and hanged, as the violators watched him shiver until he stopped breathing. Jikaranchi was left hanging by the neck in the tree, before the arsonists caught his dwelling on fire, then fled the scene.

CHAPTER
TWENTY-FIVE

When Onacona and the four Indians who went to retrieve the rifles returned home and told Chief Lakoatah and the Cherokee Council of the Horace Becket incident, the council members decided against overreacting. Even though their quarrel was against a known native bigot, none of them assumed anything of interest would come of the killing. Council members also believed that their present location was unknown to their Caucasian enemies, nevertheless, they began administering lookouts.

Chief Lakoatah recalled quite vividly the name Jonathan Becket, but had no idea he had become such an influential citizen in Jasper. After Jonathan and his raid posse slaughtered many of the villagers Chief Lakoatah left behind, the chief dreamt several times that his warriors again met Becket on the battlefield. The Cherokee chief would always awaken in a cold sweat prior to the end of the battles, wherein he envisioned his warriors being annihilated by cowboys and soldiers.

With the decision made to stay the course, the biracial brothers left their home early the following morning, and rode to consult with their friend Jikaranchi. During the young warriors' upbringing, it was he who taught them certain traits about the white man, and why they should never trust them.

Nicco and Coyote felt concerned and responsible for Jikaranchi losing his domesticated Wolf, so they brought him a replacement pup from a litter in their village. The blazing inferno and thick smoke that destroyed the Half Indian's cottage had subsided, but even before the brothers reached their destination, they suspected something was wrong.

When the Cherokee Warriors found Jikaranchi hanging from the tree, emotions immediately overcame them, from their many years of friendship. They gently lowered his battered corpse, removed the noose from around his neck, then dislodged several tree branches to construct a wooden cot. It was essential that the warriors checked the property for clues to determine who committed the crime. After close inspection they determined how many horses were present, and the number of cowboys involved, by the hooves and boot prints found around the area. It was imperative that they provided Chief Lakoatah with distinctive evidence, and buried their friend at the same time, so they prepared Jikaranchi's body for transport.

The young warriors attached the cot carrying their friend's body to the back of Nicco's horse, then dragged him back to their village. A crowd formed behind them as they rode through the village, with concerned locals who knew what the dead body meant. When they reached Lakoatah's teepee, the chief heard the excitement and came out. Once Lakoatah saw the covered over corpse, he walked over and removed the covering from the face. The young warriors left the noose atop the body for everyone to see how he died; thus, the sight angered every Cherokee. There was nothing necessary to say after everyone saw the battered corpse, thus, Chief Lakoatah led the burial procession to their ancestorial grounds, where they laid Jikaranchi to rest.

The reality of their predicament became evident, therefore, after they buried Jikaranchi the brothers rode to the location where they buried the handguns; and retrieved them. They were not expert handgun handlers, but they understood they must grasp the concept quickly, hence, they began practicing by taking apart one of the weapons. Condensation from being buried a long time caused a bit of rust, but the holsters protected the vital parts of both guns. Once they learnt how to dismantle and assemble the weapon, they faced off against each other in a quick draw contest, to increase each other's drawing speed.

The next training exercise the brothers practiced was shooting, however, like everything else they did, they were extremely competitive. For Nicco and Coyote, competing against each other helped them to master whatever challenge they encountered. To conserve on bullets, they only fired a few shots at difficult targets, to determine who had the better aim. When they finished practicing Coyote headed directly home to assist with his new son. Nicco told his brother that 'he was going for a ride to clear his thoughts,' but instead rode to Becket's Ranch to snoop around.

It was dark when Nicco reached his destination, where he left his horse to roam freely about outside the northern fence, while he snuck onto the property. The Indian crawled from the outer fence, and remained low to the ground, to avoid being seen. The first building structure the trespasser came upon was the employees' lounge, which had cowboys enjoying their leisure time-off by gambling cards, drinking, smoking, and cooking. Nicco snuck by their quarters and made his way to the main house, where he could clearly hear an aggressive tone male speaking.

Nicco snuck close to a window and peeked inside the residence, where Jonathan was speaking to several cowboys. The instant Nicco saw Mr. Becket in his expensive robe and watched his demeanor, he knew Jonathan had to be the boss. Mr. Becket was smoking a cigar and held aloft a glass of liquor, as if he were preposing a toast. The native Cherokee rested his hand on his firearm and thought of executing him right there, to alleviate all his pain. While contemplating shooting the mayor, the warrior withdrew his pistol and pressed the nozzle against the glass. Jonathan had his back to Nicco, therefore, killing him would have been rather easy, but that was not the Cherokee's way.

"I just received this here telegram from General Bailey at Fort Adams, which confirms that he will be here within two days, to help us deal with our new Cherokee problem! Great job burning them houses gentlemen, especially making it look like them Indians did it! We will finally get the chance to wipe out every last one a them Cherokee Indians," Jonathan boasted to Quick Draw and the team of arsonists!

"Thanks boss," answered the employees as they all drank their shots of liquor!

The Cherokee tribe kept to themselves and abstained from all dealings with the white man, therefore, they had no knowledge of the arsons. The young warrior realized that the Caucasians killed Jikaranchi for revenge, after they killed Becket's son. Nicco was happy he followed his instincts, or else they never would have known of the incriminating evidence used to frame the Cherokee. The U.S Cavalry's involvement in the battle would lead to the death of some of his people and much harsher penalties than the tough sanctions they presently lived under.

Mute slammed his glass against the table after he gulped down the liquid. As the guard stared at his boss admirably, he noticed Nicco through the window. At first glance Mute thought that Nicco was about to assassinate their boss, so he attempted to save the mayor's life. The gun hand had problems communicating with his peers, therefore, he withdrew his Smith & Wesson 38mm and shot out the glass pane. Nicco had already realized that he had been seen, so he took off running toward the barn.

"What the hell you shooting at, you idiot," Jonathan shouted, before he spun around and noticed Nicco racing towards his barn?

The group of arsonists and others ran out of the house and gave chase, but they could not get as close to the barn as they wished. Nicco aimed his Colt 45mm pistol through a slot in the door and shot the two front runners dead. All the accompanying gunners scattered and quickly found cover, while recklessly shooting at the barn.

"Who the hell is that Indian; and where did he come from," Quick Draw argued?

"I don't know, but he may have heard the boss," one of the arsonists stated.

"We can't afford to let him get away then! You two, get in there and chase him out," Quick Draw instructed!

Nicco had already proven that he could hit a moving target, therefore, nobody was in any haste to test his accuracy. During the explosion of gunfire, someone accidentally shot a lantern that broke and ignited a stack of hay. With half the barn filled with dry hay and animals, the fire quickly spread and engulfed the entire structure. Nicco continued shooting at anyone who attempted to maneuver closer, until he realized the barn was on fire.

The infamous Tornado for which his father was killed, had passed away three years prior, but Jonathan kept his colt and later made him his personal horse. Every animal inside the barn including Tornado's lone offspring, began fussing and struggling to escape. Coyote accessed his chances of exiting safely and decided to use the animals help. The Native Indian ran by several stalls and opened the gates, before he opened the Alpha Horse Son's gate, then leapt aboard.

To scare the animals into stampeding, Nicco fired two shots in the air, then followed the stampeders as they busted out of the burning barn. With a herd of spooked animals barrelling towards them, Jonathan's gunners quickly cleared out of the way or risked getting trampled. Mayor Becket and most of his gunners did not see when the Indian exited the barn attached to the side of the Black Stallion. Quick Draw was the only gunner who saw Nicco attached to the horse, but refrained from shooting in fear of killing his boss' prized stallion. The moment Nicco safely exited Becket's ranch, he whistled and summoned his personal horse, which followed them home.

"Did anybody see that Indian," Becket asked?

"I did boss, and I'm afraid he took your horse! Y'all get in there and try putting that fire out," Quick Draw stated!

All the workers began fetching water and tried fighting the blazing fire. The animals that escaped with Coyote were the only survivors, from the hundreds held inside the barn. Jonathan Becket was so furious that he casted blame instantly at the Cherokee, even though they had no evidence of the warrior's tribe. The mayor felt assured that the intruder was the person who killed

Horace, and that he had returned to assassinate him. With much of his live-stock killed in the fire, Mayor Becket was not about to compound his losses, so he instructed his cattlemen 'to go out and round up all the animals that fled.' After ushering his orders, Jonathan marched angrily into his house, and passed Beth on the veranda. Jonathan thought that maybe the Indian was related to one of the men he had killed, before they confiscated Tornado.

*

The Cherokee guards were extremely alert, therefore, when they heard the horses coming towards them, they readied their weapons to defend. As Nicco approached the village, he whistled to alert the guards who he was, before someone shot him from his saddle. It was dark when Nicco rode back into the village, where he wanted confirmation about the horse. The only person he knew could identify whether the horse he stole, was the great Tornado's offspring was his father, so he went directly to their tent.

"Coyote, Coyote," Nicco called out to his brother, whose teepee was close to his family!

Nicco went into his residence but could not find his father, who was in a tribal meeting with the governing tribunal. Coyote was rubbing the stallion's neck by the time his brother exited their parent's dwelling. With such tension throughout the village, many of the residents were awake. Coyote accompanied Nicco to the chief's tent, where he waited outside with the remarkable specimen of a horse. The warriors of the village were discussing their predicament, when Nicco entered and whispered something into Walking Turtle's ear. After listening to his son, the father rose from his seat and exited with him.

Coyote was standing outside holding a torch and the black stallion, which resembled his father Tornado. As Walking Turtle laid his eyes on the animal, his face lit up as if he had seen the horse before.

"The spirit of Tornado lives," Walking Turtle declared, as he walked over and rubbed the animal!

All three men went back into the tent, where the meeting was still ongoing. When they re-entered the gathering, Nyah felt that Coyote was wrong for killing Becket's son, therefore, he began chastising the brothers.

"Had it not been for your sons' recklessness, Walking Turtle, we would have no need for this gathering! One Indian is already dead, because of them," Nyah argued!

"I support the decision of my sons! If they wish for the man who killed their fathers, to feel the pain they live with, all their lives, well so be it," Walking Turtle exclaimed!

"Since you stand by your sons, can you guarantee they killed the right man," Nyah stated?

"Chief Lakoatah, my son has return with the offspring of Tornado. This proves his words is true," Walking Turtle exclaimed!

"Speak young Walking Turtle! Tell us what you have learn," Chief Lakoatah related!

"I went to home of Jonathan Becket to kill him, but I could not shoot a man in the back. But I…" Nicco began, but then paused and he lowered his head.

"You are Cherokee warrior, tell us," Lakoatah indicated?

"This evil man, Jonathan Becket, wants to wipe out our entire tribe! He pays men to look like Cherokee, then they burn houses of white people, to make U.S cavalry join fight against Cherokee! I hear him say, cavalry with General come in two days," Nicco reported, at which everyone began chattering amongst themselves!

"Silence! These cowboys and white soldiers, tried to annihilate the Cherokee once, and wipe us from our land," Lakoatah lamented!

"I believe we can defeat this U.S cavalry, here on our land," shouted a younger warrior!

"How are we to fight iron weapons with bow and arrows? We need many more weapons," a council member argued!

"We have no choice but to fight! So, we must send the women and children far away for our people to survive," Chief Lakoatah suggested.

"They won't get very far. Plus, those Apache scouts won't stop until they track them down and kill them, Walking Turtle declared!

"Our tribe must survive, and we have no tribe without the people, so we must go to Mexico! The white man will never stop hunting the Cherokee, so the Cherokee must move away from among the white man," Coyote suggested!

"These have been our lands for generations, we shall not abandon them! If we must die, then we die right here on our land, fighting, with the spirits of our ancestors" argued a council member!

"I believe my son is right. The tribe is the people, and there are many other places we can survive," Walking Turtle commented.

"That will not be possible, with all our old and young people," Lakoatah said!

"What if we find a way for everyone to escape," Nicco questioned?

"Cherokee warriors; prepare for war," Chief Lakoatah instructed!

CHAPTER TWENTY-SIX

General Benjamin Dwyer and his second officer in command, Sergeant Carter Clovers, led a security detail of a dozen men towards the Town of Jasper. Benjamin was older than the young commanding officer he was during the Cherokee's last uprising, so his hair, beard, and moustache were all grey. The cavalry commanders left their main army unit of a hundred and sixty-eight men, some three miles away from town, then rode in to speak with Jasper's elected mayor. It took the U.S Cavalrymen five hours from their base, to reach their campgrounds just outside of Jasper, however, they were well prepared to execute their mission.

The general vividly remembered the men they lost during their last encounter with the Cherokee, and how close they came to being defeated. Therefore, instead of simply depending on their Gatlin Submachine Gun, he also brought along a few bundles of Dynamite. Benjamin would often boast to his younger understudy about the adventures he had with General Warren Bailey. General Bailey had recently retired and was enjoying his civilian life further south, with his wife and dogs.

"You know I can remember this here ride like it was just yesterday! General

Bailey and I led a few men into town; and was they ever scared. People was all over us, like we had just liberated their town or something! That was a historical day Sergeant, last time I recall any Indians from these parts acting up," General Dwyer exclaimed!

"How many Cherokee Indians did y'all kill sir," Sergeant Clovers asked?

"Must a been hundreds by my recollection! General Bailey and I fought so many huge battles, that it's hard to keep the exact numbers at times," General Dwyer declared!

Days after his arrival in Jasper, Lacquary began hearing rumors circulating about 'the United States Cavalry.' The Cherokee spy contacted some friends who lived in the small Indian community outside of the town, which enabled him to avoid suspicion and blended in. The Indian Lacquary contacted, provided him with food and dwelling, which allowed him to operate in town without raising any suspicion. The female he stayed with told him about her husband, who was forced to help some cowboys one night, but never returned. According to the Cherokee female, she reported the incident to the sheriff, but nothing else came of the case.

Jasper had become a much different town from the one General Dwyer remembered. The borders of the town had expanded, and there were far more residents, homes, and businesses. During their last visit, the entire town was like a ghost town with all its residents locked away inside their homes with fear. Under the current threat, the town folks had shooters on top of the roofs and elsewhere, to protect their citizens. There were a lot more activity than their last visit, and the citizens appeared less tense than they did nineteen years prior. The town folks still expressed their joy in seeing the cavalrymen, hence, they emerged from businesses and residents to greet them. Mayor Becket and Sheriff McCall were awaiting the general outside the politician's office, where they shook hands and introduced themselves.

"Welcome General, we thank you for coming! I'm the mayor here in Jasper, Mayor Becket, and this here is Sheriff McCall! I'm sorry, but we were expecting General Bailey," Jonathan stated?

"General Bailey has retired mayor, this is General Benjamin Dwyer," Sergeant Clovers answered!

"My apologies General Dwyer; I meant you no disrespect," Jonathan said!

"No need mayor, it appears a lot has changed here in town? Jasper now looks like one a them big cities down south," General Dwyer complimented!

"The town did do some growing General. Please, let's take this inside," Jonathan stated?

Lacquary hide his face beneath the brim of his cowboy hat, while he sat by the entrance of the barber shop begging. The barber shop was next door to Mayor Becket's office, along one of the less busy streets in town. The spy assumed that Jonathan would take their discussion into his establishment and found himself the best seat possible to eavesdrop on the meeting. Nobody who went by the panhandler gave him any money, due to his foul stench that offended the locals. The citizen's reaction to Lacquary allowed him to listen undisturbed, while General Dwyer and Mayor Becket spoke candidly.

A huge crowd of spectators converged outside Becket's office, where General Dwyer and Mayor Becket held their meeting. The soldiers who accompanied the general stood guard by the entrance and ensured that nobody entered. Mayor Becket did not wish to involve any of the town's businessmen in their discussion, so he could deceive the general and get his way. After the two men sat down to talk, Sheriff McCall brought them over a bottle of whiskey and two glasses. The sheriff then brought over the mayor's cigar chest, and held it open for them to chose. With both men comfortable, Sheriff McCall fixed himself a drink, then found a seat and sat while they conversed.

"I'm happy you chose to help us deal with these savage Indians General," Mayor Becket stated!

"General Bailey was a great leader, but you wanna know what his one mistake was Mayor," General Dwyer began, as he took a puff off the cigar?

"Please, do enlighten us General," Jonathan asked!

"Back when we had them Cherokee Indians on the run! He should have ordered us to slaughter them all, then we wouldn't be having this problem today," General Dwyer exclaimed!

"I fully agree with you General! How far out of town did you camp," Jonathan said, with a huge smirk across hi face?

"Bout three miles or so along the river. I can assure you Mister Mayor, this time I'll make sure them Cherokee peasants never bother another white man ever again," General Dwyer declared!

"How do you plan to find them though General? Last word we got, they had moved their entire village," Mayor Becket asked.

"Well Mayor we got two of the best damn trackers this world has ever seen; so, wherever them Cherokees are hiding, you best believe, we gonna sniff em out," General Dwyer boasted, before he poured himself another drink and drank it down!

"General Dwyer, it would truly be an honor for me if you would allow me and a few a my men to join your mighty army, for this here historical hunt," Mayor Becket asked?

"I'm sorry Mayor Becket, but we on official government business, and I ain't permitted to carry private citizens on such duties," General Dwyer exclaimed, poured another shot of liquor, and drank that down!

"I completely understand General Dwyer," Mayor Becket said.

Lacquary sat there and played the panhandler roll until things returned to normal, slightly after the general and his cavalrymen rode out of town. Once the Cherokee spy felt confident that the locals' outburst toward natives had simmered, he got up, and walked down to the town's public stable. While Lacquary stood near the stable entrance peeking inside, a visitor to the town rode up seeking overnight care for his horse. The man saw Lacquary and assumed he was one of the horse handlers, so he dismounted and paid the Indian, then walked away.

The Cherokee spy waved goodbye to the visitor, who took his saddlebag and walked toward the hotel. Once the visitor disappeared, Lacquary climbed onto his horse, and casually rode out of town. Horse thieves were imprisoned, fined, or killed when caught, therefore, the Indian kept his head lowered and slowly rode through. As soon as Lacquary got beyond the town's welcome sign, he began galloping back to his village to warn his entire community.

CHAPTER
TWENTY-SEVEN

Every Cherokee Indian of the Nevada tribe came together that night in the middle of their village, to discuss how they would proceed against such a threat. Lacquary disclosed everything he had witnessed in Jasper, and told of the Caucasians detestation for them, whereby, they had no interest in whether they committed the crimes. When the spy finished issuing his report, many of the villagers questioned how they could be condemned, without any evidence. General Dwyer's extermination plans sent shockwaves through the tribe, thus, everyone began murmuring among themselves, before Chief Lakoatah silenced them. Lakoatah saw the fear in the females' and children's eyes, therefore, he felt compelled to try and save them.

"If we are to die when these white eyes find our village, them our bloodline must survive! I want the women and children ready to leave for the east before sunrise! The warriors will stay behind and fight these white soldiers! These are my final commands," Chief Lakoatah emphasised!

"No! Chief Lakoatah please, we don't have to die or separate! What if we had ways to all leave here safely," Coyote stood and shouted?

"Look around you Coyote! We have one reality! I too wish it was not so, but we have no choice, so we must deal with what we have," Chief Lakoatah declared, at which Coyote bowed his head in acceptance!

Instead of their typical quiet evening the entire camp was in an uproar as families scrambled to prepare the females and children for departure. Coyote had other ideas and grabbed his brother, Maharuk, and Lacquary, knowing he only had a short amount of time to arrange the items necessary for the solution he proposed. As they reached their horses and leapt aboard, Shadaiia ran up to her horse and climbed aboard, with the intention to accompany them.

"Shadaiia go back, help your sisters and mother! We can not bring you along," Coyote demanded!

"You my brothers, I know you all up to something! I am coming, and that is final! I will not run away from battle, because I am female," Shadaiia stated!

Coyote knew his sister could not be convinced against whatever she decided, therefore, he looked to Nicco, Lacquary, and Maharuk for help, but they simply shook their heads in response. They all rode away from the village led by Lacquary, who brought them to the place where the United States Cavalrymen had pitched their camp. When they reached the campground, they abandoned their horses and sent them back home by themselves. The camp was huge with the hundred and eighty soldiers stacked into several tents, which spread across a large patch of land. Apart from the guards on duty most of the soldiers were sound asleep, thus, the Indians scoped out the layout and formatted a plan, before they proceeded.

The Cherokees' plan was extremely aggressive, whereby, they sought to steal many horses, a few rifles, and a wagon to transport their babies and elderly. There were six guards on duty around the entire camp, most of whom were fatigued and dozing off at that late hour. None of the guards expected any interference from outsiders, so they paid little attention to the perimeter. Several small fires burnt throughout the camp, where the soldiers had gathered and amused themselves prior to retiring. Many of the soldiers left their rifles outside their tents stacked against other rifles, due to the small sleeping quarters they were provided.

With their plans arranged the five intruders crept on their stomachs into the camp, where Nicco slowly moved toward one of the nodding guards. The guard was leaning against a tree with his eyes almost closed, when Nicco came up behind him, grabbed his mouth shut, then thrust his knife into his back. To avoid alerting anyone, Nicco helped the guard's body slowly to the ground, and positioned him to portray someone who was asleep.

Maharuk was crawling toward a guard through some tall and course grass, when the man suddenly got up and started walking toward him. It was dark out on the prairie and the guard could see little in the distance, but he kept his focus straight ahead. The guard stopped a few paces ahead of Maharuk, starred up at the moon as he withdrew his penis, and began urinating close to the Indian. After he was through the guard went back to his seat and sat, at which Maharuk continued to press closer. The stalking Indian crawled to within three feet of the guard, then paused, looked around to make sure he was not being watched, before he grabbed the man from behind, and stabbed him several times.

The killing of those two guards allowed Shadaiia and Lacquary to move freely toward the horses, which were the Indians primary targets. The horses were stationed approximately fifty yards from the soldiers' camp, so stealing the lot would be an easy task. The soldiers tied two long pieces of ropes between four trees, after which they tied their horses' reins to the ropes. All the saddles had been taken off the horses, but they still had the bridals attached.

While Lacquary and Shadaiia loosened the ropes from the trees, Coyote and Nicco tried to confiscate a few rifles for their peers. The two least alert guards on duty were both stooped on one knee playing a card game, thus, they heard nothing when their comrades got killed. Their inattentiveness allowed Coyote to sneak up behind one of the guards, while Nicco took aim to assassinate the other. Coyote came up behind one of the guards and covered his mouth, before he stuck his knife into the man's back twice. The second of the two guards grabbed onto his pistol handle and froze, before he fell forward with an Ax stuck in his back.

The other guards on duty were stationed at the other end of the camp, so they had no idea what was transpiring. Nicco and Coyote quietly proceeded to remove several stacks of rifles from the nearby tents, with whatever ammunition they could find. Some of the horses had begun fussing in an agitated manner as if something was startling them.

A guard stationed at the other end of the camp heard the fussing horses and thought that it was peculiar at such a late hour. The curious guard left his station to check and ensured their horses were not being attacked by some carnivorous animal. By the time Nicco and Coyote finished collecting the rifles, Shadaiia, Lacquary, and Maharuk had organized the horses, and were attaching a pair of lead horses to a wagon. The brothers placed the weapons into the wagon and were debating going back for more, when the inquisitive guard fired a shot at them.

Shadaiia from nowhere fired an arrow that struck the guard in his chest, which allowed them all to climb aboard their individual transports and departed. The female Indian first climbed into the wagon Box and used the reigns to whip the horses into a gallop, as soldiers began pouring from their tents. Many of the army personnel fired at the thieves, who were audacious enough to steal from an armed brigade of soldiers. Coyote, Nicco, Lacquary, and Maharuk were forced to hang off the sides of their horses to avoid getting shot, while they dragged the ropes onto which the horses were attached. The Indians rode away under a barrage of gunfire with a hundred and fifty-six U.S Cavalry horses, a wagon, and other items which far exceeded their expectations.

It was almost daybreak when the group of bandits returned to their village, where moments before the tribe held an emotional farewell gathering. Walking Turtle, Shushuni, Makayla, and other family members were concerned about their wellbeing, having been forced to separate. The villagers assumed that the trampling sounds of the approaching horses were the U.S Cavalrymen, hence, panic ensued as many began fleeing into the woods. Many mothers sought safety with their children, while others armed themselves with either the few weapons they owned, or their farming tools. As the Indians prepared to fight, they began hearing familiar alert whistles, which pronounced who the visitors were. Once the Cherokee warriors realized who the horsemen were, everyone exhaled exhilarating cheers, knowing they had the chance to flee from their tormentors. After the horses got rounded up and warriors noticed the United States brand mark on some of the animals, they all broke out in laughter and cheered, knowing exactly from where they came.

When the team of horse thieves reached their village and began handing out the stolen rifles, Shadaiia discovered they had also stolen most the soldiers' rations. There were canned foods, bags of potatoes, and other eatable items underneath a tarp, plus barrels of water that would benefit them during their travels. Shadaiia was about to leap from the wagon when she noticed a white sac in the corner and checked its contents.

What Shadaiia found inside the sac surprised her, considering there were four bundles of Dynamite and a box filled with .30 Cartridges for their Winchester Rifles. The bullets were given out to those with rifles, however, Shadaiia hid the Dynamite bundles and gave them to her brothers. The realization that Coyote and his associates, went beyond the call of duty to provide them a better option, brought everybody together. Even though the villagers knew they were still in terrible danger, a chance at survival was all they required.

"You have all done well, especially you Coyote; and proven to this old warrior that the time has come for your generation, to lead our people to our new land! I am an old man now, but when I am no more, I hope the people appoint a leader who is as caring as you have shown, by your sacrifice for your people," Chief Lakoatah exclaimed!

"I will always serve the people of my tribe, and whoever sits as chief," Coyote responded!

"Your grandfather and I was great friends! We would roam across these valleys, just as I have watched you, roam across these valleys with your brother! Our young Cherokee warriors have always been brave, but your bravery, far surpass all that I have seen! Your father, mother, and grandfather would be proud! Just as we are proud," Chief Lakoatah stated!

The passing of the torch from one chief to the next generally occurred during a huge ceremony, still, even though that was not an inauguration, the moment felt like the passing of the baton. Coyote had never met any of his biological parents, therefore, he felt honoured that Chief Lakoatah would mention his ancestors. Knowing the strive it took to get him to that point and understanding the contributions of his native Africans throughout the years, gave Coyote the passion to help his tribe. From the stories told by Walking Turtle of his personal experiences, Coyote despised discrimination and bigotry, which was how certain Caucasians dealt with his people.

"We must leave now Chief Lakoatah, these white eyes will be coming to reclaim what we have taken! But they will show no mercy," Laquary exclaimed!

"This land has been our home, for hundreds of years! Our ancestors fought and died, to defend these grounds, on which you stand today. But these lands were here, long before the Cherokee, and they will stay, long after the Cherokee, has moved on. As a tribe, we are one people, the efforts of these young warriors, have shown me that, we must stay as one! A malicious army moves towards us, so we must do everything possible, to survive for the memory, of our ancestors! So, we will follow, Warrior Coyote's lead, and move the tribe south, into Mexico," Chief Lakoatah explained!

"Yeh-yeh-yeh-yeh," continuously yelled the tribe members!

Lakoatah raised his right hand after a few seconds of cheering, at which everybody simmered down.

"Everyone, we leave now," Chief Lakoatah instructed!

Without any enquiries or arguments every child, woman, and man capable of handling a horse was given a mount, whereby, those unable climbed onto the wagon. Walking Turtle pulled all his children together and spoke with them for a brief minute.

"Nicco and Coyote, I have taught you boys from you were young enough to fight! I know that the survival of our people depends on you both; and I would have it no other way! Remember to outsmart your enemy, and always remain one steps ahead! Daughters, it is up to us to protect the people no matter what, we shall not surrender," Walking Turtle declared, at which they all hugged as a family!

Every Cherokee knew their future was uncertain, therefore, those related to the warriors who had the task of protecting the group, gave their emotional farewells. Makayla brought Coyote's son for him to embrace and offered his departing sentiments, before she wrapped him in a sheet, tied him to her back, and climbed aboard her horse. Shadaiia went to Maharuk before he boarded his horse, at which the two simply held hands and stared into each other's eyes. Following an intense stare, Maharuk climbed aboard his horse, yet maintained their eye contact until he rode away. After centuries and generations of family raised in Nevada, nobody questioned their destination choice. Everyone was however deeply saddened they were being forced to abandon the land of their heritage.

CHAPTER
TWENTY-EIGHT

Mayor Becket and his wife Beth stood to the right of Horace's casket, while the pastor stood at the head of the grave. The mourning parents made their employees dig a grave underneath a huge tree on their property, where they selected to bury their troublesome son. The only other attendants at the funeral were Jonathan's employees and George, who all stood on the left side of the coffin. Mrs. Becket and some of the employees wept continually, while Mr. Becket maintained a stern stare.

After the pastor said his final words, he began singing "The Lord is My Shepherd," with Beth's assistance and some of the workers. The only thing Jonathan thought of was getting his revenge for the killing, despite Horace's lawbreaking lifestyle. The mayor despised Native Indians, so the thought of his son being killed by one deeply angered him. To refrain himself from shedding a tear, Mayor Becket walked away from the graveside before they started lowering the casket.

As they walked back to the house, Jonathan was remarkably silent, which was genuinely a bad sign for others. The boss stopped on his veranda to smoke a cigar and think, while Beth proceeded into the residence. It was early in the morning, yet Jonathan had already been drinking, so he withdrew his liquor flask from his inner jacket pocket and took a swallow. Quick Draw and the rest of Becket's murdering guards stood around in the yard lingering, while they awaited their boss' orders.

*

General Dwyer felt insulted by the robbery, however, the theft of United States property gave him the authority to kill on sight, any Cherokee Indian he deemed guilty. When Benjamin learnt that the wagon stolen contained most of their food rations, in addition to the explosives he gave their sergeant for safe keeping, he became so enraged that he went directly to his tent. Early the next morning the general and a small detail rode to Mayor Becket's ranch.

Added to his detail for the first time were Jackal and Shamar, one of which was close to retirement from the army. The age distinction between both scouts was evident, therefore, Jackal had long grey hair and wrinkles on his face. While approaching the house, General Dwyer took note of the destroyed barn, which was nothing but a pile of burnt rubble. As the soldiers rode up, the guards moved off to the side, and allowed Mayor Becket and General Dwyer to talk. Beth was inside her living room drinking a glass of wine, when she noticed the cavalrymen approaching, so she walked out and stood by the door.

"Morning Mayor," General Dwyer greeted!

"Morning General! I thought you would a been on the hunt for Cherokee by now," Mayor Becket stated, while staring at the Apache scouts?

"Well last night we unfortunately had an incident, where we lost nearly ninety-five percent of our horses and supplies," General Dwyer declared.

"Now how the hell did something like that happen to a well-oiled machine like the U.S Cavalry," Mayor Becket joked, at which his guards began laughing?

"About a dozen a them damn Cherokees Indians, broke into our camp last night; and stole them after killing a few of my men," General Dwyer responded!

"Well I'll be! Sneaky little bastards now aren't they? As you can probably tell by my destroyed barn out yonder? But to what do I owe the pleasure of your company this fine morning General Dwyer," Mayor Becket enquired?

"I would like to replace those stolen horses, the rations we lost, and get all the rifles you got," General Dwyer asked?

"And how do you know that I can fulfill that order general," Mayor Becket asked?

"I would not be here if I did not know you could deliver, Mayor Becket," General Dwyer argued!

"I might be able to arrange all that providing we come to the right terms,"

Mayor Becket reasoned!

"What is you proposing mayor," General Dwyer questioned?

"See back in town when we talked, I neglected to mention that them Cherokee savages, killed my only son! Since then, they burnt down my barn, killing most of my cattle, and stole one of my prize possessions! Now all I am asking for is the chance to ride along with your army here; so as, I can settle up with them savages," Mayor Becket explained?

"I'm afraid we can't put civilians in harms ways mayor," General Dwyer stated!

"As mayor, I'm no civilian general! Plus, me and the boys pretty handy with the iron, we'll manage," Mayor Becket declared!

General Dwyer could have gone through the proper protocol to reacquire the equipment they lost, but to avoid all mentions of him being ridiculed by Cherokee Indians, he had no choice but to accept Jonathan's deal.

"You got a deal mayor," General Dwyer responded!

"Have you got a list with all the rations you need," Mayor Becket asked?

"Sergeant," General Dwyer summoned, at which the cavalryman moved forward and handed Jonathan a piece of paper!

"Splendid General! I trust we understand each other when it comes to the resolve of these savages," Mayor Becket insinuated?

"We are in agreement Mayor," General Dwyer answered!

"Pleased to hear general! I'll round up those horses, plus the rest of your order, and bring em on by round midday," Mayor Becket indicated!

With their business arrangements settled, General Dwyer and his security detail turned around, and rode back to their campground. They arrived to find the crew of grave diggers finalizing the last hole for the guards who were killed on duty. General Dwyer left Sergeant Clovers to dismiss their guard detail, while he went directly to his personal command tent. A young private was present to take control of his horse, which allowed the commander to callously ignore the animal.

"Private, tell the scouts Jackal and Shamar report at once to my tent," General Dwyer commanded!

"Yes Sir, General," the private answered!

General Dwyer went into his tent, took off his coat and threw it on the chair. There was a basin containing water with a folded towel on a small table, that Benjamin used to wash and dry his face. After cleansing himself, Dwyer walked over to a huge map of the region, which laid across his desk. While looking over the map the two scouts that Benjamin sent for walked into his tent, and stood at attention.

"Jackal and Shamar reporting General Dwyer," Jackal introduced themselves!

"At ease men! Come over here and look at this map... Now last recorded settlement of these Cherokees put them around here. Figuring they somewhere else on their reservation, they could be anywhere around these parts, or these parts. Soon as these horses and supplies reach here, I want both a y'all on that trail! More than anything I'd like to find these people before nightfall. Am I understood," General Dwyer instructed?

"Yes Sir, General," Shamar and Jackal answered!

"You're dismissed! Tell Sergeant Clovers to get in here," General Dwyer stated!

"Yes Sir," answered the scouts!

Seconds later Sergeant Clovers walked into the General's tent and stood at attention.

"Sergeant Clovers reporting Sir," the Sergeant answered!

"Get the men ready for funeral services Sergeant! And have a few a them prepare a temporary barn for them horses! I'll be out shortly," General Dwyer instructed.

"Sir, yes Sir," Sergeant Clovers responded before departing!

Moments later as the Bugle Horn sounded, the General exited his tent and got escorted to the gravesite, by two guards carrying rifles. Sergeant Clovers had the entire regiment aligned and standing at attention, with the Bugle Blower positioned at the head of the pine wooden caskets. A few of the soldiers could be heard sniffling having lost associates they considered brothers, hence, General Dwyer stepped to the helm and first stared at the Pine Caskets.

"Dear Lord, this morning we gather to bury our brothers in arms! Private Baker, Private Calhoun, Private North, Private Shyers, and Private Winker were on duty last night, when a bunch a cowards crawled in our camp and killed em! Later today Lord we will be going after the cowards who did this killing; and when we get there Mighty God, I want y'all to remember what they done to these soldiers! The Good Book tells you an eye for an eye, so no matter which one a them savages you see at the tip a your rifle, make sure you remember what they done to your brothers! Lord God I ask that you grant us the strength to crush these savages and wipe them off this land; so, these five soldiers may get their revenge for the injustice done to them! All these mercies we ask Dear Father, Amen!"

"Amen," shouted all the troops!

"Amazing grace…," began General Dwyer, before everyone else joined in the singing. "…how sweet the sound, that saved a wretch like me…!'"

Twenty soldiers moved forward and lowered the five caskets into the holes, while the others continued with the singing. General Dwyer stood over the proceedings until the soldiers began tossing dirt into the holes, at which he departed and walked back to his tent under guard. Sergeant Clovers and the other troops saluted the general during his departure, then stayed by the graveside until the holes were covered over, at which they were dismissed. Following the ceremony, nobody saw or heard anything from General Dwyer, until a guard yelled 'there were horses and a wagon approaching!'

Jonathan Becket, Quick Draw, Mute, Junior, Ralph, Bobby, and two other employees guided a herd of horses into the army camp. The cowboys were scattered around a hundred and sixty horses; and brought along a wagon that carried the remaining supplies. Several cavalrymen assisted with the horses and led them into a rope-made barn, following which they were given water and allowed to graze. General Dwyer pleasantly greeted Jasper's Mayor and thanked him for honouring their deal, then led him into his command tent where they partook of a few drinks.

While the senior ranked personnel spoke in private, Jackal and Shamar exited camp to commence their tracking duties. The moment the soldier's replacement equipment arrived, everybody began preparing for departure, by dismantling tents, extinguishing fires, loading weapons, packing their belongings, and readying the horses. The mayor's companions kept to themselves, and thus drank and smoked while the soldiers worked.

As soon as everything and everyone were ready for transport, General Dwyer was made aware by his second in command. When the general exited his quarters, the soldiers were already aboard their horses, so he climbed onto his horse, and rode to the front of the line. The supply technicians quickly folded General Dwyer's tent, then packed it on their wagon. Once the general received word from the sergeant that 'he could proceed,' he sounded the advance and led them from camp. General Dwyer was joined out front by Mayor Becket, followed by the second commander, the cavalrymen, their supply wagons, and finally Becket's gunners.

Following a couple hours in their saddle, some of the troops began developing uncertainty they would find the Cherokee village. Their concern was debunked when Shamar reported back to General Dwyer, with news that reinvigorated their fighting spirits. The scout returned and informed their commander, 'that they had found the Cherokee village,' which was well hidden. The human trackers kept their distance, once they located the village, to avoid alerting the residents. There was no movement throughout the village, and the fires had burnt to ashes, so the scouts thought it might have been an ambush.

Jackal kept watch while his partner left to summon their commander. When General Dwyer and his soldiers got within two hundred yards of the village, Benjamin, the mayor, and Sergeant Carter left the troops idling and moved closer for a better look beside Jackal. By the time they reached Jackal's lookout point, the veteran Apache scout had been there for approximately an hour. There was not very much daylight remaining, therefore, they the general used his Binoculars to survey the village. After General Dwyer surveyed the village, he decided to call an all-out attack, so he instructed his troops to prepare to attack. Once the soldiers were prepared to attack, the general ordered their bugler 'to sound the horn!'

As soon as the horn sounded, the cavalrymen and civilians charged at the village, with their weapons at hand prepared to kill. The soldiers' adrenaline for slaying natives, sparked many of them to begin shooting into teepees, as they rode into the village. The Indian's mangy dogs were the only creatures seen fleeing, as some of the soldiers and cowboys dismounted their horses, then ran into several tents. After they searched through the entire camp and found nothing, Jackal and Shamar began looking for tracks. The army trackers looked along the outer boundaries of the village, where they found the Cherokee tracks pointing south.

"General Sir, these tracks show many leave to the south! Look, you can see the wagon very heavy, this make them go slower," Jackal reported!

"How far ahead are they," General Dwyer asked?

"Almost half day General," Jackal answered!

News of the attempted escape angered all the men, who felt disrespected and cheated by the Indians, therefore, they burnt every teepee to the ground. Following their destruction of the village, the cavalrymen and cowboys sat out to catch the Cherokee Indians, who were miles ahead.

CHAPTER
TWENTY-NINE

Before Mayor Becket left with the horses and supplies requested by General Dwyer, he rode into town to collect several items from his store. Sheriff McCall was supposed to attend Horace's funeral, but he had gotten drunk the night prior, and slept through it. When the sheriff awoke laying on the cot inside the jailcell, he slowly got to his feet and walked over to the hot coffee pot. McCall had a huge headache, so he poured himself a cup of coffee, then went over and sat behind his desk. The sheriff found himself some tobacco and a piece of paper and rolled himself a cigarette. As he lit the cigarette and took his first haul, Deputy Marks and Deputy Blank walked into the jailhouse.

"Morning Sheriff," Deputy Blank said!

"Morning Sheriff," Deputy Marks stated!

"I thought you was heading to Horace Becket's funeral this morning," Deputy Blank declared, as he walked to the coffee pot and poured two cups?

"God damn it! Must a slept right through it. Luckily, Mayor Becket won't be in town for a while," Sheriff McCall responded.

Deputy Blank brought Eli a cup of coffee and gave it to him. "Ah, the mayor is over by his supply store," Gus declared.

"What," Sheriff McCall exclaimed as he jumped to his feet and ran to the window?

While the deputies sat around drinking their coffee, Sheriff McCall hurried through the door. The sheriff walked down to Becket Supplies Store, where the guards were loading the supplies onto the wagon. There were nearly sixty horses all over the street being managed by Becket's cattlemen. As he approached the general store, McCall nodded his head to his associates and went in, where the boss was instructing everyone what to do. By the tone of his voice, Jeff could tell that Jonathan was in a bad mood, so he tried being polite.

"Morning Mayor Becket," the sheriff greeted!

"So, I take it you a bit too important to attend my boy's funeral," Mayor Becket stated?

"I'm sorry Mister Becket, but I---," Sheriff McCall responded!

"Blapp," sounded the slap across Sheriff McCall's face!

The sheriff gently rubbed the side of his face, then flinched when Mayor Becket pretended, he was about to strike him again.

"Don't you ever forget who made you what you are! I will take that badge off your chest, and replace you just like that," Mayor Becket threatened!

"Yes sir, mayor," Sheriff McCall answered!

There were two ladies inside the store who witnessed the disciplinary action taken by the mayor. Sheriff McCall felt terribly embarrassed, therefore, he stood beside Mayor Becket with his head lowered. After the mayor concluded instructing his employees, they walked out to the horses, where Becket climbed aboard.

"We got some unresolved business to handle, so I may be gone for a few days. Make sure you keep everyone in line until we get back," Mayor Becket declared, before they began driving the horses and wagon out of town!

After Becket and his entourage departed, Sheriff McCall turned and noticed the two women from the store staring at him. The sheriff knew the gossipers would be slandering him throughout that day, so he walked to the jailhouse and got off the streets. Moments after he re-entered, both deputies left to take a stroll around town, and left him alone. Sheriff McCall sat behind his desk and took out a half bottle of liquor from the drawer, then poured some into his coffee cup.

*

The pastor who spoke at Horace's funeral rode his single horse wagon back into town, and immediately opened the door to his church. The old woman who cleaned the church was at the front door waiting, with her broom and other cleaning supplies.

"Morning Miss Haze!"

"Top of the morning to you pastor! Seems like you had an early morning?"

"Yes ma'am, had to run out and bury the Becket's son, Horace!"

"That poor family, must a been hard for the mayor's wife losing both her sons."

"I believe it was, she was very emotional at the funeral. But Mayor Becket sure looked preoccupied, might a had something to do with them army fellows who visited with him."

"You reckon they fitting to go after them Cherokees again? Word round town is them Indians supposed to be on the war path!"

"I've had enough of all the killing here in Jasper! The good lord made us all to live as one," the pastor said as he walked to the pulpit, knelt on both knees, and began praying.

Miss Haze hurried and finished the cleaning, then said goodbye to the pastor and slowly made her way home. While walking home, the church cleaner stopped and gossiped with everyone she knew about Mayor Becket. By evening there were several rumors circulating about the mayor, who most people wanted out of office, but were all scared of him.

*

The sheriff had come under heavy scrutiny after killing the gold prospector, who many people said, 'had only fallen on bad times and was simply mouthing off!' After a few early shots of liquor, Jeff awoke at dusk with his head rested on his desk. Neither Deputy Blank nor Deputy Marks were present, so he wiped away the drool from the side of his mouth and sat back in his chair. Sheriff McCall instantly developed the taste for more liquor, so he poured out the small amount left in his bottle and drank it down. To ignore the harsh scrutiny being given to him, Jeff drank more than he normally did, so he got up and walked down to Becket's Saloon.

The atmosphere inside the saloon was loud and rowdy, until Jeff pushed the swinging doors and walked in. Everyone turned and began staring at the sheriff, who felt uncomfortable and lashed out.

"What the hell is you all looking at? Piano man, play something," Sheriff McCall ordered!

The piano player instantly began playing again and everyone went back to whatever they were doing. The bartender placed a glass and a bottle of Whiskey at the sheriff's favorite seat by the bar. Sheriff McCall poured himself a drink, then sat and began drinking. There were a lot of people inside the saloon, some whom Jeff recognized along with several visitors. As the sheriff surveyed the crowd, he took notice of a poker gambler, who tried to hide his face with his cowboy hat.

Sheriff McCall continued drinking, while he maintained close watch on the gambler. After a few shots nearly two hours later, the sheriff tried getting up from his seat, but staggered initially. Once he regained his balance, he walked over to the poker table and stood across from his suspect.

"You," Sheriff McCall stated!

The young man kept his head lowered underneath his hat and refused to look up. Sheriff McCall placed his hand on his pistol handle and got ready to draw. Everyone inside the saloon began moving away from the confrontation, as the establishment got extremely quiet. Deputy Blank was walking by the saloon when the joint went unreasonably silent. Fearing it might had been a robbery, the deputy backed up against the wall outside the bar, then peeked inside through the crack in the door.

"I ain't gonna tell you again to get out of that chair," Sheriff McCall threatened!

Everyone else moved away from the poker table and left both men across from each other. Deputy Blank walked into the saloon the moment he noticed their sheriff was involved. Sheriff McCall was focused on the gambler he was harassing, so he had no idea his deputy had entered the facility. Following the Sheriff's final warning the gambler slowly stood up, but kept his head lowered and made the hat shield his face.

"Raise your head so I can see your face," Sheriff McCall ordered!

The gambler slowly raised his head, at which everyone realized he was only underaged, and should not be inside a saloon.

"Hell, it's only Lester's boy," a customer shouted from across the room!

Several people began laughing at the sheriff, who was not in the mood to be teased.

"Who the hell is y'all laughing at," the sheriff fired back, at which the young gambler tried to put his cards on the table.

From the corner of his eye, Jeff saw when the gambler moved, but thought the youth reached for a weapon. The sheriff pulled the trigger and accidentally shot the young gambler in the stomach. When Sheriff McCall realized what he had done, he began blaming the male who commented prior.

"You are the one who caused this," Sheriff McCall declared as he turned his weapon onto the customer!

The sheriff began walking toward the commentator, who realized he was in danger and began trying to move away. Sheriff McCall fired a shot at the resident, who got struck in the shoulder as he tried running to the door.

"It's everyone of your fault," Sheriff McCall began threatening, as he turned his firearm at other customers!

Deputy Blank realized his sheriff had to be restrained, so he crept up behind him and clobbered him on the back of the neck with the butt of his hand pistol. Sheriff McCall fell to the ground unconscious, hence, the deputy went and checked on the injured gambler. The young man was bleeding profusely and thought he was going to die. To stop the bleeding, Deputy Blank removed his handkerchief from around his neck and pressed hard on the wound. One of the hoars who worked at the saloon went over and began helping with the terrified gambler.

"Please help me, I don't wanna die, I don't wanna die," the young gambler continued saying!

Instead of waiting for the doctor to come to the young lad, Deputy Blank ordered two men to pick him up and rushed him over to the doctor's home. The disappointed deputy placed Sheriff McCall in handcuff, and brought him to the jailhouse, where he locked him inside a cell. Deputy Marks was at jailhouse when his colleague brought their staggering sheriff in.

"Why you locking up Sheriff McCall," Deputy Marks asked?

"Our good sheriff here, just shot Lester's soon to be seventeen-year-old son in the gut," Deputy Blank stated!

"Let me out of this cell Deputy, y'all know Mayor Becket ain't gonna stand for this," Sheriff McCall instructed!

"The mayor ain't gonna take too kindly to you locking up the sheriff," Deputy Marks declared!

"Well then, that's the mayor's problem! But Sheriff McCall going before the judge come morning," Deputy Blank exclaimed!

CHAPTER
THIRTY

The Cherokee Indians travelled at a modest pace in comparison to the men chasing them. Survival for the Indians meant that the younger warriors would have to handle the security duties and maintained distance between themselves and the cavalry. To ensure they would not encounter any unforeseen dangers, the Cherokee tribe deployed four teams of scouts, in all four directions. Having been falsely accused of crimes they did not commit, in addition to the stolen items taken from the United States Cavalry, were assurances the Indians would be hunted. Knowing their only means of survival was to reach their destination, the Cherokee tribe pressed forward to the border.

Nicco, Coyote, Lacquary, and Maharuk all took the most dangerous direction to monitor, which was against the Caucasians in pursuit. The wagon that carried their elders, pregnant females, and those unable to ride, advanced at a modest pace, so the young warriors needed an idea of their pursuers' speed. The close friends rode back several miles and found an area up in the mountains, from which they watched the Apache scouts. The scouts were moving along rather hastily, considering the Cherokee's tracks were rather easy to follow.

The Cherokee warriors timed the distance between their convoy and the U.S scouts, knowing the cavalry would be within a mile of their trackers. At the rate with which the scouts approached, the Indians developed serious doubts they would reach safety, before they got caught. Coyote and his associates had several tactical maneuvers they thought of trying versus the cowboy, but with two well trained Apache guiding the soldiers, their chances to succeed was slim. Regardless of their perception, the Cherokee warriors had to do something to lengthen the distance between them.

All the warriors thought the two Apache scouts were the leading force behind the cavalry. To get rid of them the tribe protectors decided to use a hunting technique, they often employed when catching carnivorous animals. With the cavalrymen following several minutes behind their leading scouts, the Cherokee warriors knew they had a small window to execute both Apache trackers. The four friends rode to a location that they thought was ideal for an ambush, where there were many trees, a slight slope off the main route, and adequate shading that provided camouflage. Maharuk was to serve as the enticing bait and thereby get the trackers to pursue him. Two of the other three Cherokee warriors hid along the trail, and waited until they went by, to eliminate their most imminent threat.

Coyote and Nicco handed their horses' reigns to Lacquary, who carried the animals up the slope and out of sight. Nicco quickly climbed a tree with his holstered weapon buckled around his waist, his knife tucked in the other hip, a bow and quiver strapped to his back, and a bundle of rope over the left shoulder. The Native Indian hid where it was difficult for anyone to see him and tied a noose onto one end of the rope. From the ancient stories told by Walking Turtle of the Apache scouts, Nicco knew they were talented warriors. However, as representatives of the United States Government, they had to pay for their past crimes against the Cherokee people.

Unlike his brother, Coyote hid approximately forty yards away, among some tall trees along the woods. There was a three-foot tree stump near the wood's frontline, where the remains of the tree laid close by. The African Cherokee was also armed with his holstered Six Shooter buckled around his waist, an axe tucked into the back of his gun belt, a knife tucked into his opposite waist, and his bow and quiver strapped behind his back. Both Nicco and Coyote knew their friend's life depended on their execution, so with one chance only they could not afford to fail. Coyote's choice of weapon was his knife, therefore, he armed himself and got ready to pounce on his opponent.

Maharuk sprung his trap two miles away from the ambush location. Even though the U.S army scouts moved along quickly in pursuit, Jackal and Shamar expected the Cherokee Indians to attempt some sort of trickery. Jackal knew their adversaries were devious warriors, who could deceive them into assuming they were headed in a different direction, so he paid close attention to the tracks.

While approaching a mountainous area, the U.S trackers were surprised, when Maharuk leapt out from the wooded area and began galloping away. The Apache scouts were approximately ninety yards behind, so they assumed they crept up on a scout who probably fell asleep, and thus gave chase. The fleeing Indian kept his head lowered and rode hard, with the scouts on his trail firing their hand pistols at him. General Dwyer and his soldiers heard the faint gunshot sounds ahead and immediately increased their travelling velocity, to ascertain why were the shots fired.

Maharuk did as instructed and rode directly underneath the tree in which Nicco was hiding. Moments thereafter, the bait galloped by the bushes in which Coyote waited patiently for his target to pass. A short time after Maharuk went by, Shamar galloped pass the tree in which Nicco hid, in his haste to catch and kill the escaping Cherokee. As soon as his senior partner Jackal came along, Nicco who had one end of the rope secured to a tree branch, lassoed him around the neck beneath the tree. The horse that Jackal rode continued galloping on, but the veteran scout got yanked from the animal with such force, that his neck snapped instantly.

Shamar had no idea what happened to his partner and continued chasing the presumed scout. With gunshots zipping by overhead, Maharuk kept his body lowered onto his horse, and trusted his brothers in arms would accomplish their duties. As Shamar rode by, the camouflaged black Indian placed the blade of his knife across his mouth and held it with his teeth. The Apache scout was so focused on Maharuk, that Coyote unexpectedly ran from the shadows, leapt on the tree stump, and used his velocity to clothesline Shamar across the neck. The forceful impact knocked the scout off his horse and sent him crashing to the ground. Shamar's pistol went flying across the plains, nevertheless, he painfully pranced to his feet and quickly withdrew his knife. Coyote fell and summersaulted a short distance away, before he removed his knife from his tooth's grasp, and prepared for hand-to-hand combat.

"My ancestors should have wiped your kind from these lands! But after the white man kill all your tribe, your people will be no more," Shamar threatened!

"None of that matter Old Man, because that day, not you, nor your partner will be there to see it," Coyote answered, before he charged at the Apache!

Sparks gashed as the two Indians' knives smashed continuously against each other. Despite his age, Shamar was still quite skilled in combat and defended himself extremely well, versus the younger Indian's continuous strikes. Both men stabbed at each other and fought to gain an advantage, until Coyote made an error and got his arm caught in a twist. The Apache forced Coyote to drop his knife, then tried to plunge his blade into the African Cherokee. Coyote grabbed onto his hand and tussled for control, before Shamar stumped him in the chest, which sent him crashing to the ground.

"Old Man you called me! How old is that, little boy," Shamar teased, as he walked in to finish the job?

Coyote rolled backwards and pounced onto his feet, just as Shamar lunged forward and tried to stab him in the chest. The well-trained Cherokee grabbed onto the Apache's hand, then twisted it downwards, before he bent back the wrist, at which he heard the bone break. The knife dropped from Shamar's palm to the ground, but the scout was far from defeated.

Shamar fought through the pain, as he grabbed onto Coyote's long hair, yanked back his head, and tried to put the younger warrior in a chokehold. The Cherokee warrior could ill afford being put in such a devastating hold, so he jammed his fingers into Shamar's left eye. Both warriors fell to the ground and rolled away from the knife, during which Shamar climbed atop his opponent and hurled down three punches at him. Coyote was very flexible, so he used his right leg to wrap around Shamar's neck and dragged him off, thus, separated them both temporarily.

The Apache Indian still had no idea what happened to his partner, but he was fortunate to find a knife beside him once he finally regained control. When Coyote began climbing to his feet, he saw Nicco taking aim at Shamar with an arrow from behind. Even though Jackal was strung up and left hanging, in the distance, the sight of the dead Apache inspired Coyote. To stop his brother from shooting, Coyote waved his hand at him and signal him, therefore, Nicco lowered his bow. Shamar would have gotten shot in the back with the arrow, but Coyote was opposed to cheating in battle.

"Like I promised you; you and your army traitor will not live to see us dead! Look, see yourself, your friend is already with the spirits," Coyote stated while pointing at the hanging scout!

Shamar stupidly looked around and was shocked at the sight of his long-time mentor hanging from a noose. Coyote wasted no time to attack and speared Shamar with a devastating shoulder tackle directly to his mid section, which caused him to drop the knife. The Cherokee warrior could hear his opponent grimaced in pain as they crashed to the ground, where Coyote flipped behind Shamar and placed him in a chokehold. Thoughts of his ancestors whom the Apache scouts led their Caucasians friends to kill, went through Coyote's mind as he squeezed the life from Shamar's body. Nicco and the other warriors rode up with Coyote's horse, at which he released Shamar from his death grip, picked up his knife, then they all fled the scene.

CHAPTER
THIRTY-ONE

Deputy Blank and Deputy Marks nervously sat loading every weapon they had on the rifle rack against the wall. There were different boxes with the various size of bullets being loaded, on the sheriff's desk. None of the deputies knew what to expect from Mayor Becket when he returned, so they both prepared for the worst. The front door to the jail had been bolted shut, and the deputies had several loaded rifles underneath the window, ready for a shootout.

"Somehow I always knew it would come down to something like this," Deputy Marks declared.

"Tragedy brought me to stop in Jasper, but the nice folks in town made me settle down here! Since then, the only problem I seen is Mayor Becket, and them gun hands who work for him," Deputy Blank stated!

"Well, first thing I'm gonna do come morning is send that telegram, requesting that Governor Casey come to Jasper," Deputy Marks exclaimed!

"I want you to be careful out there! A lot a people in this town is on Becket's pay role, so you gotta see everyone as a threat," Deputy Blank instructed!

"Y'all can plan all you want, but sooner or later you gotta go outside this here jailhouse to get food or something! How long y'all reckon you can hold back all then gunners," Sheriff McCall argued?

"Shut your mouth Sheriff," Deputy Marks lamented!

"You best listen to me Eli, don't follow this dead man and end up in a pine box beside him," Sheriff McCall reasoned!

"He just mouthing off deputy! Trying a save his own skin is all," Deputy Blank exclaimed. "Karma has a way of showing up when you don't expect sheriff!"

"Not ever the wrath of god is gonna save y'all from my friends! You both dead! You hear deputies? You both dead," Sheriff McCall threatened!

A knock sounded at the door which startled Deputy Marks. Deputy Blank grabbed a loaded Double Barrel Buck Shot Rifle off the desk and cocked both hammers. Deputy Marks withdrew his Smith & Wesson 38mm handgun and prepared to open the door.

"Who is it," Deputy Marks whispered with a high tone?

"Your cousin Nate," the male at the door answered!

Deputy Marks slowly unbolted the door lock and snuck a peep through the crack. When he saw that his cousin was alone, Eli opened the door and allowed his entry.

"Did you tell everyone what I want them to do," Deputy Blank asked?

"Yes Sir, Deputy Blank, everybody will be in position," Nate responded, before Eli allowed him back through the door and bolted the lock!

*

Mayor Becket's employee at the General Hardware Store was inside the sa-loon when Sheriff McCall got taken into custody. After the young gambler got taken to the doctor's house, and Deputy Blank took the sheriff away, things slowly returned to normal. Almost everyone inside the saloon began com-menting on the incident, which they expected to be the start of something much larger. Warren did not want to give the impression that he had his boss' best interest in mind, therefore, he proceeded with the preposition he had been offering a whore. Both Warren and the whore were seated at a small table in the corner of the saloon, where the female sat on the store clerk's lap. They had been drinking and enjoying the festive atmosphere, despite the mishap that occurred.

"Come on Lisa-Mae, I swear I'll pay you the other half soon as Mister Beck-et pays me for working over by the store," Warren pled?

"The service that I provide is a business, so you best make sure that once you get paid, I get my money! Since we at an agreement, let us take this upstairs," Lisa-Mae stated!

They both got up from their seats and began walking toward the stairs. Lisa-Mae began up the steps, but Warren headed directly to the entrance instead.

"Where the hell is you going," Lisa Mae demanded?

"Oh, I forgot the money in my other trousers, I'll be right back," the store clerk responded!

Everyone inside the saloon began laughing at Becket's employee, who walked out of the saloon.

"Don't you ever set foot in this here saloon again, you worthless piece of," Lisa-Mae shouted, before she stormed up the stairs!

Warren walked out to the hitching rail, untied his horse, climbed aboard, then rode straight out of town. Beth Becket was having difficulty sleeping; therefore, she was drinking a glass of Brandy inside her Living Room. The grieving mother walked around with a framed photo of Horace, while she drank, smoked, and spoke to herself.

Warren rode onto the Becket's ranch and rode up to the main house. The property was extremely quiet with nearly everyone gone, so the store clerk was concerned if he would deliver his message.

"Mrs. Becket, Mrs. Becket, Mrs. Becket, Mrs. Becket," Warren continuously called out!

Beth grabbed her husband's Colt Shotgun and walked out onto the porch. The store clerk heard when the lady of the house yanked back the hammer on her rifle, therefore, he threw both hands in the air.

"It is Warren from the hardware store ma'am! I work for Mister Becket," Warren shouted!

Beth slowly approached the cowboy who sat atop his horse. Until she found out his reason for being on her property at such a late hour, Beth kept the weapon pointed at Warren.

"What can I do for you at this hour of the morning Warren," Beth demanded?

"Ma-am, Deputy Blank arrested Sheriff McCall for shooting Lester's son," Warren explained!

"Oh, that's terrible! Was Lester's son killed," Beth asked?

"I don't know Mrs. Becket! They rushed him over to the doc's place," Warren commented!

"Well, I guess Jonathan's gotta have to sort all that out once he gets back," Beth stated, as she lowered the rifle.

"I gotta head back Mrs. Becket! Just had to let you know so you can tell the mayor once he gets back," Warren said, before he turned his horse aside and rode away!

CHAPTER
THIRTY-TWO

By the time the cavalry reached where their Apache scouts got ambushed, Coyote and his companions were long gone. The soldiers were astonished that the Cherokee warriors specifically targeted their trackers, without whom the Indians exact directional heading could be misjudged. Should they experience any unforeseen weather such as heavy rain, whereby the tracks washed away, they would have no chance of finding the Cherokee Indians thereafter. Even though all the evidence suggested that Chief Lakoatah was defecting to South America, General Dwyer knew the Indians were proud Americans, who would never surrender their land. Continuing from that point was a humongous gamble, however, people with bruised egos such as Mayor Becket would not accept that resolution. Most of the soldiers shared the mayor's sentiment, plus none of them wanted history to record their humiliating defeat at the hands of Natives.

"Somebody cut that man down from that tree," General Dwyer immediately ordered!

"How the hell did they manage to get Jackal strung up like that," Sergeant Clovers exclaimed?

"Them new generation of Indian savages ain't no dummies Sergeant! I've personally seen them in action; and the best thing we can do to keep them in line, is make sure they stay on those reservations," Mayor Becket declared!

"What do you think Sergeant? Think we could still track Chief Lakoatah," General Dwyer asked?

"General if we lose them and they disappear we'll never find them! For all we know them Indians could be trying to clear out them tracks up ahead, so we best be at em while those tracks are still fresh," Sergeant Clovers responded!

"I'm willing to wager that them Indians are trying to ride for Mexico! Only problem is, they got children, pregnant women, and old folks to care for, so long as we hurry, they will never get there before we catch em," Mayor Becket reasoned!

"These Indians are smarter than we think General! To steal our horses and supplies, is something nobody would ever plan for," Sergeant Clovers declared.

General Dwyer thought to himself for a minute. He recounted their conflict from years prior, when his unit of soldiers was chasing the Cherokee warriors. The general remembered how difficult it was for their professional trackers to locate the tracks, so he knew they needed help. The Apache village was approximately twenty-five miles South-East of their location, thus, Dwyer thought he could employ new trackers.

"Sergeant, I want you to press on with the rest of the men! I am going to take a small team and bring the bodies of those trackers back to the Apache nation. Hopefully, we can get some replacements for them," General Dwyer insisted!

"Sir, yes Sir! You men are with the General! The rest of you, prepare to ride," Sergeant Clovers exclaimed!

"That is insane General! They are savages who can't be trusted," Mayor Becket warned!

"Mayor Becket, there have been many Native Indians who served this United States of America army long before I was born, and they will continue to do so," General Dwyer responded!

General Dwyer had them tied both scouts to a horse, took some condiments from the supplies wagon, then rode off toward the Apache village. The main trail south went around Apache land, so it was possible for General Dwyer to divert off the route, and still catch up to his soldiers along the way. A dozen soldiers rode behind the commander as they went into the Apache village, dragging the horse that carried the dead scouts. Many Indians quickly gathered around the soldiers, before they parted the way and allowed their chief to approach.

The Apache chief unwrapped the blanket used to cover the scouts' bodies, to ensure they were deceased. When some of the ladies saw the dead Indians, they began weeping and calling out. An Indian took the horse's reigns from the soldier holding it and brought it away. General Dwyer dismounted off his horse and addressed the Apache leader.

"Great leader of the Apache nation, I am General Dwyer! I must again thank you for allowing the service of your great warriors, Jackal and Shamar! This small gift is a token of our gratitude, for what your talented scouts did for this nation! These great trackers were ambushed by Cherokee warriors, fleeing for their lives! The United States Army must catch this group of rebels, who stole our horses and food! I am seeking with your approval, two or three strong trackers, who will help us locate these criminals," General Dwyer stated?

"General, before the white man come to our land, to the north lived Indians, to the west lived Indians, to the south was Indians, and to the east lived Indians! After your people drove us all from our lands, now every direction I look, I see the white man! Still, today you come here asking for Apache help, to find another tribe of Indians, who you wish to remove from their land! No General Dwyer, the Apache shall not help the white eye this day," the Apache chief said!

"I ask you to reconsider Great Chief? The United States Army has always helped the Apache," General Dwyer argued!

"I have spoken General Dwyer, the Apache will not help you to find these Cherokee," the Apache chief declared!

There were warriors in the crowd who had interest in accepting the general's preposition. Despite their interest in an army career, those warriors remained silent, knowing they had to abide by their chief's decision. After years of a solid partnership, General Dwyer felt disrespected by the Apache chief's decision. With that the army commander climbed back into his saddle, and led his troops off the reservation, toward the main army.

*

Sergeant Clovers and the rest of soldiers continued on the trail, hoping to close the gap between the Indians and themselves. It was believed the Cherokee were not too far ahead, by their desperate attempt to send the army commanders into disarray. The tracks left by the Cherokee were still detectable, but the soldiers knew that mother nature could have quickly changed everything.

The four Cherokee scouts separated and formed two teams once they eliminated the Apache scouts. There was a pivotal area approximately seven miles ahead, where the Cherokee warriors thought they could reduce the number of soldiers and disrupt their route. The warriors believed they could block the pathway at that location and force the cavalry to find another way through. At the selected location, the trail narrowed and passed between two extremely tall cliffs, which were blanketed with huge boulders and sharp rocks. If the

Cherokee warriors could stop the cavalry from passing through the valley with their wagons, the soldiers' only alternative would be to turn around and take the long way around. If successful the maneuver could provide the Cherokee Indians the separation they needed, to safely reach the borders and entered Mexico.

Coyote and Lacquary found a safe position for their ambush atop the eastern slope, while Nicco and Maharuk chose the identical location on the opposite cliff. Both teams preplanned their methods of assault, knowing they would not be able to vocally correspond thereafter. In case any of the teams had difficulties, the warriors contingency plan was to use hand signals to warn the other. The Cherokee scouts arranged to explode the dynamite they stole along both sides of the cliffs. Even though they only had a few bundles of dynamite, they hoped it would be enough to cause a landslide that would block the trail, and possibly eliminate some of the soldiers. Without Match Sticks to spark the Dynamite's Fuses, the Indians gathered some dried bushes and clashed lime stones together to create the fire. It took Lacquary much longer than anticipated to engineer the fire needed to light the fuse, so Coyote held up a fist and signalled his brother to wait. Sergeant Clovers and his troops were several yards away from galloping through the designated strike zone, when both scout teams finally got their fuses lit.

"Kaboom," sounded the bomb planted by Maharuk and Nicco! The explosion blasted chunks of rocks from the hillside and started the rockslide that the scouts hoped it would. Seconds after the first eruption, the other explosion sounded and caused a similar landslide.

Sergeant Clovers and his soldiers were cautiously advancing through the passage when the bomb sent panic waves through the regiment. By the time the bombs exploded the commanding officers were in the danger zone and could not turn back. At the eruption of the first bomb the cavalryman to the front of the formation, began whipping their horses for the animals to gallop and clear the danger. All the commanders and nearly thirty cavalrymen safely made it pass, while another hundred and one soldiers were fortunate enough to stop and avert the danger. The remaining soldiers perished in the landslide, with the wagon that carried the soldiers' tents and other supplies. Had Coyote and Lacquary been ready when they originally planned to ignite the explosives, they could have done far worst damage than they accomplished.

During the landslide Nicco and Maharuk began shooting down at the distracted soldiers, who were trying to save themselves. The soldiers were scattering and could not return fire, so the Indians took advantage of the free target practice. Maharuk fired seven shots and managed to kill three soldiers, while Nicco who was a much better shooter killed five men and only fired six bullets. The driver of the wagon carrying the high-powered Gatlin Gun, was spared because he loitered behind with Becket's gunners. Therefore, once he observed his retreating comrades getting picked off by the shooters, he prepared the submachine weapon and began returning fire.

Maharuk was focused on the leading batch of soldiers and did not notice the wagon handler, assembling the Gatlin Gun. When Nicco spun toward the submachine weapon and saw the soldier, he yelled out to Maharuk, then hid behind a huge bolder. His partner could hardly hear a sound with all the loud explosions, thus, he failed to seek protection. Bullets from the high-powered weapon bore through the warrior's chest and killed him instantly. Nicco dropped his weapon and moved to his friend's aide, as Coyote and Lacquary began dowsing the soldiers below with bullets from their location. The first soldier Coyote shot dead was the man mining the Gatlin Gun, who had managed to disrupt their perfect plot.

While checking his companion's vitals for a pulse, Nicco protected himself behind a huge bolder. The powerful Gatlin Gun was no longer a threat, so he knew he had to take advantage of his chance to escape. After Nicco ensured his partner was deceased, he grabbed for Maharuk's Winchester Rifle, then took off running with his head lowered. After seeing all the debris caused by the Dynamite, Coyote felt confident they had done enough damage to hinder the soldiers. Both sides exchanged gunfire, during which Lacquary and he killed thirteen soldiers, before they withdrew from the shootout and made their escape.

CHAPTER
THIRTY-THREE

The crowd of Apache that gathered transported their deceased warriors to their resting place. The families of both scouts were all present, to usher their loved ones off to the spirit world. Their chief presided over the burial, during which he was enraged that none of their scouts ever made it to retirement. Despite their chief's comments, Calian and two of his friends thought otherwise of the U.S Army; and wanted to help with the hunting of the Cherokee Indians.

Shamar's cousins Adahy and Benquasha, shared Calian's sentiments, so they stood together throughout the funeral procession. Contrary to other villagers, these warriors grew up in families where they heard many stories about their siblings' heroics, thus, their passion for the army was unlike any other. While everyone grieved that evening, all three men plotted to leave their village later that night, once everyone had gone to sleep. The mourners were up until late that night celebrating the memories of their beloved villagers, who brought their families and tribe prosperity.

Many Apache believed that the aide supplies they received from the U.S Government annually, was because to their scouts' involvement with the army. Due to the scouts' service to their village, most of the community grieved with the entire families. As family members, Calian, Adahy, and Benquasha were also honored by their villagers, who held a huge fest to blessed them. It was extremely late when the three Apache warriors finally snuck away from their village to join up with General Dwyer, whom they believed would lead them to wealth and adventure.

*

After they left the Apache Village, the General and his security detail were on course to rendez-vous with the main army, when they heard the dynamite explosions. The loud explosion frightened General Dwyer and his soldiers, who began riding even faster to reach their comrades. General Dwyer felt immediate regret not being with his soldiers during such a confrontation, trusting the Indians possibly used the dynamite against them. Various scenarios began floating through the army leader's thoughts, as they drew closer to the bullet exchange.

When General Dwyer and his guards got within a quarter mile of the battle, the shooting suddenly stopped. The devastation the commander saw grieved him when they arrived on the scene. All of the soldiers were in rescue mode as they fought to retrieve those wounded from among the rubble. Everyone pitched in and tried to help, including General Dwyer and Mayor Becket, who did not lose any of his gun hands. It took the soldiers a while to rescue those trapped, hence they were able to pull four men with serious injuries from the pile of boulders. The field physician examined the soldiers then reported his diagnosis to the general.

"General Dwyer the men all sustained serious injuries, so most of them will not survive a trip back! The best I can do for them right now is give them something for the pain, but I am afraid they all will not live much longer," the medic declared!

"Do whatever you can for em Doc! Our rations have been cut short again, so we ain't got much," General Dwyer said!

"But General Sir, what about the men beneath the rubble? Ain't you gonna make some men dig them all out," the medic enquired?

"Doc, I got more than half of my squadron on the other side a that there rubble, so my priority is getting this unit back together! I want all these soldiers to save every ounce of strength they got! Cause come tomorrow we fitting to catch them Cherokees; and when we do, they gonna unleash all the fury they got on them Indians," General Dwyer emphasised!

Despite being embarrassed thus far, the cavalry's fighting moral was surprisingly positive. In fact, the bodies of the deceased soldiers and those injured, inspired their comrades to press on and complete the mission. The soldiers and cowboys on the other side of the rubble were ordered to turn back and circle around the mountain, which took them several hours. General Dwyer felt terribly disappointed when he looked over at the soldiers pinned beneath

161

the rubble and those who grimaced in pain from their injuries. However, he could clearly distinguish the look of determination in the other troops' eyes. With the soldiers and cowboys all eager to proceed, General Dwyer gathered his Senior Officers and Mayor Becket to orchestrate a strategy. Their map of the territory and other essential supplies were destroyed in the supply wagon, therefore, the general found a piece of stick and used it to illustrate in the sandy soil.

"After the men catch up to us, we give em a few hours to rest up! Their horses also need the rest, but we ride before daybreak gentlemen," General Dwyer declared!

"Now you talking general," Mayor Becket stated!

"The Apache will be no help to us, but I figure that Chief Lakoatah is heading straight south for Mexico! Now, we gotta ride hard and fast to catch em after this holdup, but long as we get an early start, I believe we can catch em," General Dwyer lamented!

There would be no funeral procession for the soldiers crushed by the rock avalanche, hence, to show their respects several of their friends knelt by the pile of bodies and prayed privately. General Dwyer paused for a few seconds when crossing back the debris; and bowed his head in a small prayer before he continued. The Medic went back to treating the injured soldiers, some of whom were rendered paralyzed due to fractured spines and other broken limbs. Due to insufficient medical supplies the level of aide the medic could administer was minimal, so he gave each soldier a Morphine Injection for the pain. When checking one of the soldiers' vital signs the doctor discovered that the man had succumbed to his injuries, and thus sent word to inform the General.

"I want guards over yonder, up there, there, and up there! I want y'all alert at all times tonight, understand me," General Dwyer ordered?

"Sir, yes Sir," the soldiers answered!

With each passing moment waiting for their separated comrades the soldiers grew increasingly vengeful, not having their usual supper and other amenities that brought them relief, at the end of long grueling days. Without the comforts of their tents, the cavalrymen were forced to deal with the elements outdoors, therefore, they built several bond fires and grouped together around them. Coffee was one product of which they had no shortage, but the soldiers were forced to snack on whatever items they could find. Mayor Becket brought his own food, so he camped separately from the soldiers, cooked a meal for his men and himself, then ate.

The stranded troops went back from which they came and around the mountain to reconnect with General Dwyer. While awaiting the troops' arrival, General Dwyer lit a cigar, as he surveyed the landscape. The general knew that Chief Lakoatah selected that specific route to avoid confrontations with some of the mid-west most vicious Indians. Tribes such as the Berry Creek Rancheria of Maidu, the Big Pine Paiute Tribe, and the Bear River Band, were all enemies of the Cherokee. Any form of trespassing on another native reservation would have been construed as an act of aggression, and thus was assured to start a war.

When the separated soldiers and cowboys reached the camp, they were exhausted and falling from their horses. The cowboys were abled to replenish some of their strength by eating, but the soldiers were physically drained. Despite needing long rest, General Dwyer only allowed the soldiers and cowboys to sleep for only three hours, before the wakeup call sounded. Even though there was a huge chance the soldiers would perform less than admirable, the general chose to take that gamble, rather than have the Cherokee Indians escaped.

CHAPTER
THIRTY-FOUR

Nicco, Lacquary, and Coyote respectfully brought their friend's horse back to camp. It was impossible for them to recover Maharuk's body under assault from the Gatlin Gun, so they fled without him. They had all been friends since childhood and grew like brothers, therefore, they all felt a genuine sense of responsibility and sorrow. The tribe of Indians camped as a tight group around several small fires, instead of spreading out across the large terrain. There were several intermediate armed guards between them, and other guards further away from the camp. By the time Lacquary, Nicco, and Coyote reached the Cherokee's camp outskirt, the area was extremely dark. To safely enter their camping grounds, they whistled a specific chant to alert the guards.

Some of the villagers were resting for another long day of travel, with hopes of reaching their destination by late afternoon. When they left Nevada, many of the Indians doubted they would survive the one-thousand-nine-hundred-and-thirty-nine-kilometer journey to Mexico, but with only a few hours of travel remaining, they grew increasingly confident. There was a festive atmosphere among some of the Indians, most of whom felt assured they would reach safely.

The joyous mood quickly changed when the scouts rode into camp with

Maharuk's horse. Several females began weeping instantly, while some of the young warriors fought to hold back their tears. Being on the run meant they would not have the time to properly appoint their fallen warrior to the realm of their ancestor, yet they prayed and honored the young brave's service to their clan. The announcement of Maharuk's killing awakened everyone else, and was a stalk reminder, that they were still in grave danger.

Shadaiia had devoted her life and affections to Maharuk, so she took the news especially hard. The female warrior did not need anyone to explain why her future mate was not aboard his horse, therefore, she ran off on her own. To hide her emotions and mourn the man she cared for, Shadaiia went behind Chief Lakoatah's tent and cried silently.

Coyote, Nicco, and Lacquary had gone to Chief Lakoatah's tent, and were debriefing him and several other elders. As they began talking Shadaiia recognized her brothers' voices and began listening keenly. The scouts advised their chief of the soldiers' Gatlin Gun, in addition to the possibility they could get caught before they reached the border. The debating Indians were unaware that only a few feet away, Shadaiia who had been pouting over her loss, overheard everything they discussed.

Shadaiia heard someone coming and moved away thereafter, to avoid getting caught eavesdropping. The furious female hid in the shadows and watched Lacquary, as he walked from the chief's teepee. The scout had to relieve himself, so he walked over toward some bushes to urinate. The female warrior unsuspectingly followed, then crept up behind Lacquary while he urinated in the brushes. Shadaiia grabbed Lacquary from behind and aggressively placed him in a choke hold, following which she placed her knife against his genital, which immobilized him instantly. The disruption of oxygen made Lacquary wince, but the sharp blade pressed against his penis abruptly disrupted his urinary flow.

"Tell me where to find the white man's camp? And I will not ask again," Shadaiia demanded!

"At the mouth of small mountains, close to Big Pine Paiute Indian land," Lacquary squealed!

"We never talked, you hear me," Shadaiia angrily whispered!

"We never talked," Lacquary whispered.

Shadaiia had physically whooped Lacquary twice in the past, wherein she threatened next time to sever his manhood. Knowing she meant every word she said, once Shadaiia released Lacquary he grabbed his genital, hunched forward, and exhaling a huge sigh. The warrior female was intent on avenging Maharuk, who was the only male in their village she felt an emotional connection to. Maharuk had tried to pursue Shadaiia for years, and finally succeeded at getting her to change her boyish temperament; but the soldiers awoke the

165

beast in her.

Before setting out on her suicide mission, Shadaiia went down to the river and covered herself with mud, to offer herself some camouflage. The enraged warrior rode directly to the United States Cavalry camp, where she abandoned her horse two miles from their location and went the remaining distance on foot. Armed with her Bow and loaded Quiver, a Winchester Rifle, an axe, and two knives, Shadaiia crept closer to the cavalry camp. Before she got too close, the trained female pinpointed the guards' location, then moved in.

General Dwyer had increased the number of soldiers on duty, therefore, each guard station had up to three alert soldiers on the lookout. Each guard station was thirty yards from the actual camp, where the cavalrymen slept in groups around several fires. Instead of using her rifle, Shadaiia selected her Bow and Arrows, and her Axe as her weapons of choice, knowing they allowed her the opportunity to strike silently from a distance. To succeed at her task, the Cherokee warrior knew she had to operate quickly and decisively, thus, she withdrew two arrows and held one between her teeth. She had snuck within twenty yards of the post without being seen, due to the dark coating over her skin.

With her attack strategy devised, Shadaiia took aim at her first target, who had his back turned towards her. Shadaiia shot the guard in the back, reloaded quickly, then shot the second guard in the chest. Before the third guard could react or yell for help, Shadaiia tossed her axe directly into the man's chest. There was an overseer assigned to check on the guards periodically, who Shadaiia did not account for. The soldier walked over to the guard post and was astonished to find his comrades dead, so he began yelling 'Indians!' Even though the soldier had no idea where the intruders were, or how many of them were there, he took off running back toward their camp.

Shadaiia's dark complexion matched the darkness along the plains and made it incredible difficult for anyone to see exactly where she was. The warrior female was very nimble, so to avoid being spotted she crawled from her first location, as more soldiers began joining the defensive line. Sergeant Clovers took control once he joined the guards on alert and could be heard barking orders at some of the soldiers. While transferring to another location Shadaiia noticed a guard racing to the post where she killed her first three victims.

With more soldiers joining the search team, shooting the guard could reveal her position. Regardless of the result, Shadaiia was there to kill as many soldiers as possible, hence, she blasted an arrow into him. The force of the impact knocked the man off his feet and pitched him to the ground. Without idling, Shadaiia selected another arrow and shot the pursuing soldier, who was rushing to get out the line of fire. The arrow severely injured the soldier; however, he somehow began crawling to safety after he struck the ground.

"Over there," a soldier shouted at which several of his comrades began firing in Shadaiia's direction!

The soldiers were at first cautious not knowing exactly how many Indians they were up against, until they ascertained the danger was that of a singular threat. Shadaiia hid behind a huge bolder while the soldiers' bullets whistled by in every direction. They had managed to pin her down with limited options, but seriously underestimated her capabilities. The soldiers assumed that their attacker's only weapon was a bow and arrows, nevertheless, they exerted all precautions.

Sergeant Clovers instructed six men to circle around and apprehend the intruder, while other soldiers continued to douse the offender with bullets. Shadaiia could not maneuver to fire an arrow without getting shot, so she tossed the bow and grabbed for her Winchester Rifle. The Cherokee warrior thought she would have deceived the soldiers, who approached with caution even though they had control of the situation. As soon as the approaching soldiers were in sight, Shadaiia pointed her weapon in their direction and shot the point man in the upper arm. Every soldier who accompanied the injured cavalryman immediately dropped to the ground, at which some of them began shooting at the intruder.

"Hold your fire! Hold your fire! Hold your fire," yelled the point man even though he was nearly killed by the Indian!

A few more shots rang out before the soldiers completely stopped firing. Shadaiia had her entire body crouched in a tight ball and knew she had no choice but to surrender.

"You there, toss that weapon and stand up with your hands above your head," said the point man!

At the soldier's warning, Shadaiia tossed the rifle and raised her hands high above her head. While the female attempted to get to her feet, one of the men charged in and butted her across the temple with his Winchester. The female warrior fell to the ground, at which the soldier aimed at her with the intention to shoot, before one of his comrades held onto his weapon and lifted the nozzle to the sky. It was dark and none of the cavalrymen thought their attacker was a female, therefore, they treated the prisoner with discontent. Some of the soldiers were upset that the attacker killed their colleagues, thus, Shadaiia was kicked several times even though she was already unconscious.

Two soldiers dragged Shadaiia across the terrain by her legs and dumped her at the edge of their camp. The knife she kept on her hip was confiscated by the soldiers, who thought the Cherokee was some deranged lunatic for attacking them. There were several tall trees nearby, one of which the soldiers securely tied Shadaiia with a piece of rope. Sergeant Clovers approached the bloodied prisoner with a burning torch, to determine the person's identity, then discovered she was in fact a female. When General Dwyer heard of Shadaiia and the number of guards she killed, he went to personally see who the female warrior was. To positively identify her, the general had a soldier doused her with water, to wash away the mud. Most of the soldiers were surprised the Cherokee was a female, considering she conducted herself like a male warrior.

"You look awfully like one a dem Cherokee Squaws," General Dwyer argued!

"And you look like one of them Caucasian dogs," Shadaiia said in her Cherokee language!

"Now I ain't sure you understand what I'm saying, but if you do, you only got one chance a surviving come morning; and that is if you tell me where to find your people," General Dwyer threatened!?

"I will never tell you white eye how to find my people! We did nothing to you people, yet still you hunt us like deer," Shadaiia responded in English!

"Your people massacred innocent God-fearing white folks; and y'all gonna pay with your lives," General Dwyer angrily stated!

"The only guilty men here is you! None of us Cherokee fear your guns, or going to the Spirit World, so we will fight till there is none of us left," Shadaiia threatened!

"Then come morning you will be the first woman I put before a shooting squad! But I doubt you will be the last before this here conflict is all said and done," General Dwyer warned, before he walked away!

With everybody returning to their prior location, Quick Draw passed close to the Indian prisoner and whistled to gain her attention. The cowboy then spat on her, and signalled cutting her throat, before he continued by.

Shadaiia slowly raised her head and looked up at the bigot. "I want you to know this, before I take my last breath, I will kill you!"

Quick Draw felt offended by the comment, so he went back and stumped the prisoner in the face with his boot heel, which rendered her unconscious for a second time. When Shadaiia regained consciousness sometime after, the camp was back to normal and most of the soldiers were sound asleep. There was nobody watching her and the few soldiers who were still awake, had their interest elsewhere. Her face had a wilt from being stumped, and the blood had dried against the side of her head, but as Shadaiia looked around she knew there would be no other opportunity to escape. The beating she took was the worst she had ever experienced, but she grew up fighting with her brothers, and was a lot tougher that the soldiers thought. Regardless of what she told General Dwyer, Shadaiia knew he would execute her simply to energize his troops and inspire them to chase her people.

None of the soldiers suspected Shadaiia had any other weapons, so they neglected to search her thoroughly. The warrior female carried a concealed knife tucked in her leather sandal, which none of the soldiers noticed. Without hesitation the prisoner slowly retrieved the knife, then used it to cut her restraints. Once freed Shadaiia crawled over to some nearby bushes, where she gathered a bunch of twigs and used them to erase her tracks. The Cherokee female began making her escape, when she felt drizzles of rain falling from the clouds. Instead of escaping, Shadaiia circled back to one of the wagons, that had a tarp covering it, and hid underneath. Moments after the Cherokee female used all her strength to latch onto the bottom of the wagon, she overheard a commotion, as the soldiers realized she had escaped, and began scrambling to find her.

When General Dwyer got the briefing, he immediately ordered Sergeant Clovers to dispatch several troops to search for the prisoner. The execution of such a valiant intruder would certainly have motivated and excited his cavalrymen, so the general wanted her found. Their camp was searched extensively, before the soldiers turned their attention elsewhere. Several soldiers rode out into the rain in search of Shadaiia, whom they believed was on foot and thus could not have gotten far.

Walking Turtle had taught his children how to supress pain through meditation, therefore, while holding onto the wagon's under-carry, Shadaiia relaxed her breathing and concentrated. Once the soldiers stopped searching the camp, Shadaiia snuck into the wagon and hid beneath the tarp, close to the driver's box. All the soldiers assumed the female would attempt to get as far away as possible, so they then concentrated on the outskirts of the camp.

The unexpected rain threatened to ruin the soldiers' chances of catching the Cherokee, especially if the water washed away their tracks. During all the excitement, Calian and his two Apache friends, rode up to the U.S Army guard post, and asked to speak with General Dwyer. The guards escorted the Apache scouts to their general, who was elated they had chosen to join his regiment.

CHAPTER
THIRTY-FIVE

The town of Jasper was quiet and serene the following morning. Business owners were starting to open their places of business, but there was an unsettled feeling throughout the town. Nearly everyone had heard about Sheriff McCall's arrest, hence, they expected some sort of retaliation by the mayor, who was to return shortly from his trip. Deputy Blank and Deputy Marks sat inside the jailhouse with their prisoner, who was fully sobered up and talkative. Neither of the deputies knew what to expect while they transferred the sheriff, so they sat nervously watching the time intensely.

They were supposed to transfer the prisoner over to Judge Saunders' residence at 9:05 AM, where the decision on how to proceed would be rendered. Lester's son had passed away before daybreak, even though the doctor did his best to save the teenager's life. Deputy Marks was initially skeptical about locking up their sheriff, until they received news that the youth had died. The situation was nerve wrecking for the deputies, who could potentially have issues with Mayor Becket's gunners and Mr. Lester.

"You know it is gonna be a shame watching them shoot you both down in the middle of town! Deputy Marks I can not believe you willing to bet your life on a loser like this! If I were you, I would just let me go free before the mayor gets back! Probably when you explain what happened, hopefully he won't kill you…" Sheriff McCall exclaimed!

"How bout we pass you over to Mr. Lester and those friends of his," Deputy Blank argued?

"Now, let's not get too carried away Deputy Blank! Everybody saw me shooting that boy, was purely an accident," Sheriff McCall responded!

"Pity I don't see Lester looking at it like that," Deputy Blank stated!

At 8:55 both deputies ensured their weapons were loaded and ready to fire. They selected two Smith & Wesson Buckshot Rifles from their gunrack, then handcuffed their prison for transport. It was extremely early for a shot of liquor, yet still Deputy Marks took a drink to calm his nerves. By 9:00 AM they unlatched the door and walked out with Sheriff McCall, who was still running his mouth. They walked down the sidewalk to Judge Saunders' house, with a slew of town folks watching them from across the street.

"If that man does not stand trial for murdering Mr. Lester's boy, this whole town is gonna burn," a male standing next to Mr. Lester shouted!

The deputies kept close watch on the men who stood with the deceased youth's father. The atmosphere was intense as the lawmen made their way to the judge's residence. There were several men standing in second story windows with rifles across the street, most of whom supported the deputies. Deputy Marks and his partner reached the judge's residence without incident, then presented the sheriff before the magistrate.

"Morning Judge Saunders," Deputy Blank stated!

"Morning Deputy, you care to explain why Sheriff McCall is standing before me in chains," Judge Saunders demanded?

"Judge Saunders, Sheriff McCall shot and killed Mister Lester's teenage boy inside Becket's Saloon last night," Deputy Blank explained!

"What was the boy doing inside the saloon at them hours," Judge Saunders asked?

"I believe he was playing poker your honor," Deputy Blank answered.

"Judge Saunders it was purely an accident! I may had gotten a bit drunk and thought he was someone else, but I never meant to harm that kid," Sheriff McCall injected!

"As a man of the law the folks in this town deserve better from their sheriff! Lock him back up until trial," Judge Saunders ordered!

Their walk back to the jailhouse was none less intense than their walk to the judge's residence. News that Sheriff McCall was to stand trial soothed some of the locals, but the anomaly in the case was the absent Mayor Becket. None of Mr. Lester's friends commented during their return, nor did the deputies incurred any problems from Becket's associates. The positivity Sheriff McCall exhumed had all but disappeared upon their return, once he realized the rescue he expected was not forthcoming. The deputies knew it would be a tough trial and were unsure of the ending, still they were willing to fight for justice for Mr. Lester and the town of Jasper.

CHAPTER
THIRTY-SIX

The Cherokee scouts assigned to the other directions knew the areas they surveyed were of importance, but everyone expected their greatest threat to come from the soldiers chasing them. Despite their beliefs, they still had to protect their people from other Indian tribes, therefore, they stayed the course until they were closer to the border. There was a somber mood throughout the entire Cherokee camp that night, as most of the Indians considered whether they would survive. They had travelled a long distance, yet still had much further to go, but to reach their destination they would have to buckle down and move faster.

The African Indian walked up and stood beside his adopted mother Shushuni, then held onto her hand, and squeezed it. Without uttering a word, Shushuni's eyes filled with tears, whereby she dropped her head onto Coyote's shoulder, and began sobbing. The sun had not yet risen in the sky, but even before the Indians started their final journey, there was an eerie feeling throughout the camp.

Nicco and several warriors were secluded from the others, preparing mats made with straws. A group of warriors were selected to slow down the cavalry's charge, which was a monumental task. Before they sat out on the last length of their trip, Chief Lakoatah felt the urge to speak with his people and warn them of the possible altercation versus the cavalry. If they were to perish, he wanted them prepared to fight until the end, thus, they would never surrender.

"May the spirits of our ancestors, protect us! I wish, I could guarantee you all a safe journey, on this day; but the White Devil, who chases us, may catch us before we reach, our new home! We have many young children to protect, elders, and our pregnant mothers! This enemy carries huge Gatlin Gun, to wipe us all out, so we must ride faster! If we must fight, then we show this enemy, what it means to face a true Cherokee warrior! Have no fear my people, for the spirits of your ancestors is with us! Climb aboard your horses, we ride!"

Immediately following the speech everybody from the elderly, men, women, and children boarded their individual transport, then sat out on the last length of their quest. Many of the Indians had to be helped aboard the wagon and some onto horses that they should not have been put in charge of. However, if the youngsters from five to fourteen, and the mothers carrying babies tied to their backs were to survive, they had to use the skills taught to them from infancy. The faster pace would prove difficult especially for the pregnant females, who were the primary reason for the slow pace thus far. Walking Turtle spoke with his sons, who were scheduled to return to their scouting duties, on the most dangerous day of their travels.

"I laid to rest both your fathers many moons ago; now today we all mourned the loss of your sister! But none of you will see the Spirit World before I, so as I may tell my old friends about the greatness of their sons! I am proud to call you both my sons, the true champions of the Nevada Cherokee people," Walking Turtle stated, before he leapt onto his horse and waited for his daughter-in-law!

Makayla had Coyote's child properly secured across her chest, with her bow and quiver attached to her back. Everyone understood that they may need to fight to save their tribe, so each Cherokee was ready for the battle. The saddened female waited to say goodbye to her mate again, knowing they had already lost a family member. Contrary to Walking Turtle, Makayla was less optimistic about Coyote's return, but she believed in his talents and thought they would reconnect.

"Show them no mercy, because they will show us none! Your family will be waiting for you in Mexico! Don't be late," Makayla stated, before she turned and rode away with Walking Turtle!

Both brothers stood and watched their father and Makayla caught up to the rest of the tribe. The young warriors were smeared in their traditional war paint, which they painted onto their faces and bodies. Coyote used white paint to administer his designs onto his darker complexion, while Nicco used black paint for his designs. Armed with their holstered firearms, Winchester Rifles, bow and arrows, axe, and knives, the young braves stood prepared for battle. To ensure their horses were also prepared for battle, the young warriors

174

smeared paint patterns on the animals. The legendary son of Tornado had Nicco's handprints all over its coat, while Coyote decorated his horse with teardrops, used to represent Shadaiia.

The biracial brothers leapt onto their horses and were joined by Mata, Lacquary, Kemeshika, and twenty-two other warriors, who were all willing to die for their tribe's safety. The youngest among them was fifteen-year-old Magoonta, who chose the rare privilege to serve with the War Party. Before reaching the juvenile age, every Indian was taught combative skills, so Magoonta's bravery was encouraged without any thought to age.

The war party rode three-miles-north and found an ideal location to set their trap. It was important for them to reduce the number of troops chasing their families, even at the risk of losing their own lives. All the warriors placed the lives of their siblings and community before theirs', hence they would do anything to give their loved ones a chance at survival. There was a sizable cliff close to the location selected, from which they could obtain a clear view of the soldiers approaching. The team of warriors made Magoonta their designated lookout; and instructed him to 'watch for torches or any signs', while they prepared their trap.

It was still dark across the territory, but the warriors sought to use the decreased lighting to their advantage. Some of the warriors rode out approximately twenty yards from the cliff, where they used their tools and dug eight full body length holes into the ground. The holes dug were approximately six inches deep, but most importantly several feet away from the main trail. Each hole was placed at a strategic location, then occupied by a Cherokee warrior, armed with his loaded rifle and a handgun. The straw mats that the warriors made were used to cover the Indians, before a piece of Bamboo was placed into their mouths to help them breathe. Most of the soil was then reused to cover the ambushers and presented an illusion to whosoever passed by. Prior to leaving their comrades, the young warriors took a second to acknowledge their friend's bravery, then said their final goodbyes.

For the Indians' trap to be effective the cloak of darkness was essential, otherwise the altered terrain could have gotten spotted. Daylight was over forty minutes away and the Indians estimated the cavalrymen would be along before then. As the crack of daybreak drew closer, the Indians began wondering if they had misjudged the troop's time of arrival. Thirty-three minutes later with the slow materializing daylight, Mata decided to abort the mission and tried to cancel. Knowing their comrades could have been exposed by the brightening morning light, Mata wanted to cancel, when Magoonta pointed out the approaching scouts.

General Dwyer and his troops broke camp at 4:20 AM to provide themselves the opportunity to catch the Cherokee Indians. The entire region was pitch black when they sat out on the trail, therefore, they had to use torches and remained close to their scouts. Following a second night of attack where

175

more soldiers were killed, most of the men felt slightly vulnerable in the dark, and nervously awaited the light of the day. General Dwyer and Mayor Becket led the troops at a modest pace behind the scouts, who were still able to locate the tracks despite the rain.

Knowing they still had to conserve their horses' energy throughout the day, the scouts proceeded at a much slower pace than the soldiers expected. The cavalrymen were ready to ride their horses into the ground that day, if it guaranteed they would catch and exterminate every last Cherokee. When many of the soldiers realized that daybreak was upon them, they began feeling at eased, not having to contend with the devious Indians during the dark.

With the scouts cautiously approaching with their focus mainly on the ground, Mata thought he needed to create a diversion or risked losing his friends. The plan called for the buried warriors to strike after the soldiers had passed by. However, none of them expected the soldiers to have Apache scouts leading them. Mata thought the ambushers were about to get discovered and took aim at the leading Apache. Coyote and the rest of the war party were all hiding along the top of the cliff, patiently waiting for the soldiers to ride pass their shooters. Without any warning, Mata shot the lead scout off his horse, expecting the rest of soldiers to attack.

The Cavalry Commander noticed the suspicious uneven soil, as they drew closer to the ambush location. Mata's killing of General Dwyer's scout however took precedent, as Calian leapt off his horse, to avoid being the next victim. Once Mata opened fire his colleagues had no choice but to join in, therefore, Nicco and the other warriors at the edge of the cliff started shooting. Mayor Becket and General Dwyer followed their scout's reaction and leapt off their horses quickly. Calian's other Apache companion was also shot and fell from his horse, as the Cherokee warriors sprung their trap. The sharpshooting Indians removed four more soldiers from their horses and knocked off two additional cowboys. Some of the other soldiers and cowboys began dismounting off their horses and began shooting back at the Indians. Despite Mata's premature shooting, the Cherokee warriors accomplished their mission to slow down the cavalry.

The Winchester discharge and subsequent Apache killings forced the uniformed soldiers to break formation. As the soldiers scattered across the plains, they began moving closer to the hidden warriors. When the first Cherokee leapt from his shallow hole, he not only frightened a soldier aboard his horse, but he also startled the animal. The horse riled into the air, and tossed the soldier off its back, therefore, he went crashing to the ground. The Indian proceeded to shoot the soldier and two of his mounted comrades, before Sergeant Clovers shot him in the back. All the other ambushers leapt from their hiding places, and killed several additional cavalrymen, before they were shot dead.

The trained soldiers began using their horses as protection, as they returned fire and moved away from the gunfight. The Cherokee warriors aimed to maim the cavalry soldiers at all cost, so they shot some of the horses to get at their riders. General Dwyer and the rest of his companions moved away from the danger area, instead of prolonging the shootout. The band of Indians could not afford for the soldiers to unleash their Gatlin Gun or conjured up a plan to overpower them, so they ran to their horses and rode away.

General Dwyer ordered his soldiers to gather the scattered horses which had no riders. The General then accessed their situation to determine the number of casualties they had sustained. Two soldiers were injured with non-life-threatening injuries, therefore, the medical officer attended to them. One of the soldiers was shot in the foot and the other broke his arm when he fell from his horse. Despite their injuries, the two men were eager to get back on the chase, once the doctor patched them up. The soldier with the broke arm got his hand placed in a sling, while the wounded officer got some ointment applied, and his leg wrapped.

CHAPTER
THIRTY-SEVEN

Information about the United States Cavalry chase reached the attention of the Mexican President Pablo El-Platto. The president was willing to allow the Cherokee Indians sanctuary in his country and provide them a piece of land for dwelling. President El-Platto initially learnt of the attempted massacre by the U.S Cavalry, before it was announced that the Indians were heading south. When the President heard of the story it was told to him as a rumour, by the least likely of individuals, which was his gardener, Manuel Hernandez. Mr. Hernandez was the first cousin to Louis Hernandez, who got sent back to Mexico until his employer Mrs. Beth Becket deemed it safe for him to return. Beth gave the barn hander an adequate amount of currency and specific instructions during his absence, but Louis had the tendency to get intoxicated and yap off at the mouth.

The first event Louis attended after he returned home was the wedding of his cousin Sylvia, who was Manuel's youngest sister. It had been years since Louis saw many of his family members, so that night at the reception they all got drunk, danced, laughed, and caught up on old times. Louis and eight of his male relatives came together and chatted amongst themselves, while the rest of their siblings enjoyed the delightful festivities.

"Wow, I can't believe little Sylvia is now all grown up and married," Louis commented!

"Time passes quickly cousin. How about that girl you used to see named Margarita? She was a beautiful girl, eh," Ricardo asked?

"A year after I moved to the U.S, she married some guy named Rafael," Louis answered.

"Aunty tell us you find a good job, work for very important people like cousin, Manuel. Why you chose to come back to Mexico after all these years in America," Enricque questioned?

"My boss warned me never to mention their business and payed me to keep silent, but you are all my familia and I trust you! When I was in Nevada I worked for the mayor in the Town of Jasper. Very rich gringo, but also very brutal man name Jonathan Becket. He owned a big cattle ranch with thousands of cattle and never go anywhere without his guards. I heard stories this Mayor Becket started the Cherokee Indian uprising many years ago, by stealing a horse caught by the Indians, then he killed them to hide what happened. To get the position as mayor, Senior Becket killed people, threatened others, and paid some out of town whore, to take dirty pictures, with the old mayor! But after he turned mayor, Becket started sleeping with the same whore! His wife Beth Becket was going to fire me one day, for peeing in a horse stall; and when I begged for my job, she gave me only one option," Louis paused and wiped tears from his eyes, when he thought about what took place!

"I did not want to do it, but what else was I supposed to do!? Her husband got the whore pregnant, so she tell me to kill this woman, or else… So I ride to the place with Ramirez and left him outside, to lookout for me, break into the house, then go to her bedroom. But the whore had a gun and shot me, so I ran away! When we go back to the ranch, Senora Becket was angry I did not do the job, and send me back here until the lawmen stopped looking for me!"

"Hahaha, that story is the best you ever told cousin," Manuel joked!

"I am serious Manuel! Look, this is where that whore shot me," Louis responded then revealed the scar!

"How can you be sure that those gringos will make you come back," Enricque enquired?

"Ramirez sends me letters to keep me inform! But I do not think I will go back to work for those gringos, because in the last letter Ramirez write that a Cherokee Indian, killed their only son Horace. To retaliate against the Cherokee, Senor Becket send his murdering guards to burn and kill other innocent gringos, to trick the U.S Cavalry to get involved. Now they will go and kill all these people like they did years ago, just to save face for their son, who everybody know is a criminal! If you don't believe me, you can all read the letter I just receive from Ramirez," Louis exclaimed as he withdrew the letter from his pocket and passed it to Ricardo!

"Did Ramirez say when you can return," Enricque enquired?

"Come dance with me my son," said Louis' mother who grabbed his hands and began pulling him onto the dance floor!?

"No, but I am in no haste to return," Louis answered as he walked away!

The letter got passed to Manuel and he read it but decided against returning it to its rightful owner. By the time Louis finished dancing, drinking more liquor, and socializing, the letter was the furthest thing from his mind. Thus, Manuel was able to confiscate the letter without any objections from his cousin. The next day Manuel went to work and was trimming the plant edges along a walkway, when President Pablo El-Platto hailed him on his way to his poolside.

"Morning Manuel, comma es-ta?"

"Bien Senor Presidente, can I talk with you for one minute," Manuel responded?

"What is it my friend," President El-Platto asked?

The Mexican President had not yet received any information about the U.S Cavalry chase, nevertheless, he was more than willing to listen to Manuel who was not even a member of his National Security Team. Such an incredible story would have been hard for anyone to believe, hence, as reference Manuel gave Pablo the letter he stole from Louis. Due to the undercover intel achieved by the Mexican President, when the factual case got brought to his attention, he immediately summoned his top general.

President El-Platto held a meeting at his home with General Titto Escabar, with respect to securing their borders with the United States. The President made it clear that the Cherokee Indians were to be awarded a home, if they were to be exiled, however, the Mexican Army's duty was only to ensure that no American soldier illegally crossed onto their side of the border. General Escabar knew far less of the situation than President El-Platto, therefore, he did not see the need to dispatch the troops if they were not provoked. In response to the general, the Mexican President pointed out that it was important they played a humanitarian role in the crisis and ensured that no one got mistreated.

The General departed President El-Platto's home and went directly to his command post at Fort D'Agusto Ruberio, where they had over three thousand soldiers enlisted. Within two and a half hours following the official briefing, General Escobar had five hundred Mexican soldiers prepared to ride to the border. Among the army being deployed, were two secondary Senior Officers, three Flags Men hoisting the country's National Flag and their Units' Flags, followed by the legion of basic troops. Once everything was organized the army left the fort and went to the border crossing, where they expected the

Indians would attempt to cross over. When they reached their destination, the soldiers stayed mounted on their horses and were directed to form four rows, with General Titto Escabar and his Senior Officers delegated to the front.

CHAPTER
THIRTY-EIGHT

General Dwyer stood beside Mayor Becket and watched as the soldiers killed in the Indians' ambush were pilled together. Even though the soldiers considered their horses a valuable part of their regiment, the animals were not awarded the same humane treatment. None of the soldiers had eaten a solid meal for more than a day, thereby, they blamed the Cherokee for everything faulty that happened. While the famished soldiers worked, the surviving cowboys stood by their horses and ate Beef Jerky, as they impatiently awaited the order to proceed.

"Damn sure aches seeing people you care about get killed! Reminds me a that hurtful way I felt when them Cherokees killed my boy," Mayor Becket stated!

"That Indian was not lying about her people having nothing to do with those killings; was she Mayor Becket," General Dwyer asked?

"At this point I don't think any of that matters general! I'm sure your men will agree with me," Mayor Becket argued, before he walked over toward his guards.

General Dwyer at that junction realized they had been tricked into helping Jasper's Mayor, achieved his revenge against the Cherokee Indians. Although the general could not be faulted if he canceled the chase, they had lost more than two-thirds of their army personnel, therefore, to save face he was compelled to completing their mission.

"Sergeant Clovers, prepare the men to ride," General Dwyer instructed!

"Company fall in! Mount up," Sergeant Clovers commanded, to which everyone got on their transports!

The Cherokee warriors' horse prints were as clear as the morning, yet their lone scout quickly set out on his tracking duties.

Onward, hoo," added the sergeant once the soldiers were aligned behind the general!

Hungry with stomachs fueled by hatred, General Dwyer and the surviving members of his army charged after the fleeing Indians. Coyote and his band of disruptors had managed to terminate a few more soldiers, and gained some separation between them, so it was then a sprint to the finish. Every soldier and their cowboy counterpart were outraged, they had gotten outsmarted by people they considered as primitive. Regardless of the outcome, General Dwyer and everyone involved knew that they would be ridiculed for being embarrassed on multiple occasions. The Caucasians only constellation prize would be if they killed every Cherokee, therefore, they mercilessly chased after the Indians.

The Cherokee warriors rode fast and hard to catch the rest of their tribe members. Contrary to the day prior the Indians travelled at a faster pace, knowing the intention of the beast chasing them. It was slightly after midday when they caught the rest of their tribal relatives, but as they approached family members to those already lost, began weeping. There was no time to stop and strategize or sympathize with the grieving mourners, moreover, they still had several miles to travel before they reached the border. Despite travelling at a fast pace, the main group of Indians was advised to move much faster if they were to have any chance at reaching their destination.

Nicco caught up to Chief Lakoatah who still handled a horse extremely well despite his advanced age. The young warrior disclosed some of what happened during their morning mission and reported their number of losses. Even though Nicco provided an estimated calculation of the number of remaining soldiers, he abstained from hypotheticals when asked, 'their chances of making it safely to the border?'

Coyote and the remaining young warriors stayed to the rear of the convoy, where they expected to serve as the first leg of defense. Some of the elders' optimism had decreased since their scouts' return, which caused more murmuring among those inside the wagon. There was very little that Shiloh could do for the weaker elders and others under her care, but she did her best to make everyone comfortable. The chief's mate crawled about the wagon and assisted whosoever was in need. Several of the pregnant women were under duress from the constant harsh jerking, but none more so than Kishana who was on her eighth month of pregnancy. The Cherokee female was incredibly strong and fought to preserve her pregnancy to term, thus, she tightly latched her legs together and held a firm grip onto the wagon.

They came upon a river later that afternoon that took some time to cross without tragically losing anyone. The tribe's biggest fear had already come to fruition; therefore, their primary objective became to safely reach Mexico. Halfway across the river Kishana exclaimed that 'her water had broken!' Some of the wagon's occupants feared they would need to stop, so they refuted her claim. Two of the other pregnant females insinuated that 'the water was possibly due to the running river seeping through the wagon. After they exited the river on the opposite side, Kishana continued complaining about her stomach, therefore, Shiloh crawled over to her and examined her. During the examination, the chief's mate uncovered that Kishana had indeed began the birthing process and immediately advised Lakoatah.

The Mexican Border was only two miles away and they were only guaranteed freedom by crossing over, so everyone began encouraging her 'to hold the delivery!' General Titto Escabar watched the developments through his binoculars from their post at the border. Regardless of what transpired on American soil, the Mexican army could not interfere. The Mexican soldiers were lounging about their camp, when a horn sounded that alerted them to prepare. The Spanish soldiers quickly mounted their horses and got into formation behind their general.

A fifth of a mile removed from the river, Coyote looked back and saw the cavalrymen fast approaching the river. The African American Indian whistled to alert his partners, then stopped his horse, and turned to face the soldiers. The small group of Indian warriors all checked their weapons to ensure they were loaded and ready to discharge, before they slowly began walking their horses toward the cavalrymen. As the soldiers came across the river, Coyote locked eyes onto Jonathan Becket and his murdering guards. There was no one else who was of any consequence on his radar, so if he had to die, he hoped to take the mayor with him. Just before Coyote gave the order to charge at the U. S Cavalrymen, Chief Lakoatah, Walking Turtle, and the remaining elderly male warriors rode up alongside them.

The instant General Dwyer exited the river he began barking orders at his troops, to prepare them to defend against the Cherokees' ill-advised attack. The general sent the Gatlin Gun operators over toward the left side of the field, then assigned Sergeant Clovers to instruct the gunner. While the wagon and its two occupants went where they were instructed, General Dwyer aligned his soldiers for the final attack. The Gatlin Gun operator stopped the wagon approximately fifteen yards away, removed the tarp from the weapon, grabbed a case of bullets, and quickly loaded the machine. Before the gunner finished assembling the Gatlin Gun, the warriors began ridding toward the soldiers and cowboys. When General Dwyer realized that the courageous Cherokee warriors were attacking, he quickly gave the command for the gunner to shoot.

"Look at these pathetic fools, have no idea they are all dead men! Then we kill everything else remaining," General Dwyer lamented before he gave the signal!

The Gatlin operator began firing high impact bullets at the charging Indians, which pitched them from their horses like a strong wind blowing leaves. The Mexican soldiers watched the disgraceful massacre, yet could do absolutely noting to help the Indians. Snuggled in a corner of the wagon, Shadaiia had no training on how to operate a Gatlin Gun, so she watched as the cavalry gunner prepared and utilized the weapon. Once she believed she understood how to handle the Submachine Gun, Shadaiia crept closer to the gunner, and used her knife to stab him in the inner right thigh, close to his groin. When the gunner tumbled inside the wagon, Shadaiia held him down and stabbed him twice in the ribcage, before she withdrew his side-iron from its holster.

Shadaiia popped up inside the wagon and aimed at Sergeant Clovers, then shot him off his horse, and killed the second wagon's operator. The disruption in the sweet rhythmic sound from the Gatlin Submachine firing, startled General Dwyer who looked over and saw the escaped female Indian, in control of their secret weapon. Without hesitation Shadaiia turned the weapon against the cavalrymen and began wiping the U.S soldiers off the battlefield.

Despite being eradicated at the beginning of their attack, the Cherokee warriors never broke stride and began assisting with the soldiers' annihilation. Walking Turtle and his sons were happy to see their sister, whom they assumed had been killed. The powerful Submachine Weapon quickly eradicated a number of soldiers, thus, to escape Mayor Becket and others attempted to cross back the river. Shadaiia thought she had killed Sergeant Clovers and had her interest focused elsewhere, when he staggered to his feet, and shot her in the stomach. Nicco observed when Shadaiia got injured, therefore, he instantly shot and killed Sergeant Clovers with his rifle.

After Shadaiia realized she had been shot, she looked up and saw Quick Draw moving towards the river. The warrior female had made him a promise, so she aimed the weapon at him and squeezed the trigger one final time. Wayne Allen and Mute were blown from their saddles, following which Shadaiia released the Gatlin handle, and sat back inside the wagon. Coyote was not about to offer Mayor Becket another chance to escape and shot him off his horse, at which he fell faced down in the water and floated away. By the time all the gun-firing ceased, the U.S cavalrymen and their cowboy comrades were either dead on the terrain or washing away downstream.

Nicco rode over to the wagon where Shadaiia was struggling to breathe, and lifted his sister onto his horse, then brought her along with them. Had the Indians not been victorious their entire tribe could have been eradicated. They would have had to stop the wagon before they reached the border, to assist the pregnant female during her childbirth. The enfant delivered became the last Nevada Cherokee bore on American soil, as the survivors made it to the border thereafter.

The battle was bloody and costly, but the Cherokee Indians knew they would no longer have to deal with the racism they faced in their new homeland. Chief Lakoatah had no idea what to expect from the Mexican soldiers, but felt honored that they welcomed them without any restrictions or prejudice. The Mexican Government provided the Cherokee people with land and helped them settled into their new country, where for the first few weeks they mourned the lives of those killed. President Pablo El-Platto attended their first ceremony, during which he provided the Indians with the Land Deed and signed a Coalition Agreement with their new citizens.

CHAPTER
THIRTY-NINE

B etty Lee rode onto the Becket Cattle Ranch on a single horse buggy and proceeded up to the main house. The maid was watering the plants on the verandah, when she noticed the cart coming along the walkway, and made herself available to greet whoever the visitor was. There was far less activity around the ranch than normal, following the deaths of Jonathan Becket and several of his helpers. When the buggy came to a stop, Betty Lee picked up a baby basket from the seat and passed it to the maid.

"You best be holding that child proper, one a these days all this property and everything else is gonna be his," Betty Lee declared!

"Yes Ma'am! Who is you here to see," the maid asked?

"Beth Becket of course! Let her know that Mr. Becket's new son and his mother are here to talk business," Betty Lee stated!

The maid showed Betty Lee into the day's room and advised her that she would inform Mrs. Becket. Before she left Betty Lee ordered her to bring fresh milk for the baby upon her return, then fixed herself a glass of liquor, and made herself comfortable. Soon as Betty Lee got relaxed, she heard footsteps coming down the stairs. Jasper's newest richest man, Mister Lester, stopped by the entrance and greeted the new mother, before he continued through the front door. Mister Lester untied his horse from the rail outside, climbed aboard, and rode off the ranch. Moments later Beth came down the stairs and walked into the room, where Betty Lee awaited her arrival, with her feet hoist onto a night table, while she relaxed in the sofa.

"What an unexpected surprise! To what do I owe the pleasure," Beth said?

"You can drop the act Beth, we both know you tried to kill me and that did not work! I'm here to get what belongs to my son; Jonathan Becket's son," Betty Lee declared!

"And what makes you think you are inclined to anything? My husband is dead, so as far as I'm concerned, every bad deal he ever made died with him," Beth stated!

"This here is Jonathan's flesh and blood, so whatever I have to do to get what's coming to him, I am going to do! If that means to drag your name through the mud then be prepared, cause you ain't fitting to run me out a town this time, Beth," Betty Lee argued!

Beth walked over to the Liquor Cabinet and fixed herself a drink, then walked over to a side table as she sipped from the glass.

"It would have been best for everyone involved had you stayed where you where," Beth commented!

"I'm sure you would love that, so you can keep it all for yourself, you wicked Old Bat," Betty Lee sighted!

The maid walked into the room with a glass filled with milk.

"The milk you requested ma'am," said the maid!

"I did not ask you for any milk," Beth exclaimed!

"I told her to bring it for the child," Betty Lee interrupted!

"She works for me, you don't boss my help around," Beth insisted!

"Come, come now Beth, we both know all that is bout to change! Here child, pour it in this here bottle," Betty Lee declared!

"Let her have the milk and get out," Beth ordered!

The maid placed the glass on the night table and exited the room. Beth took one of Jonathan's old cigars from the table drawer and lit it ablaze.

"I see you have acquired Jonathan's taste for cigars," Betty Lee reasoned.

"Don't you ever mention my husband's name ever again," Beth threatened!

Betty Lee fixed the child's bottle and took him from his basket, then proceeded to feed him. Beth smoked across the room and stared at Betty Lee with utter despise, while she played around with the baby in her arms.

"What name have you given the boy," Beth questioned?

"His name is Adam Jonathan Becket! Isn't he the handsomest thing you ever seen," Betty Lee proudly responded, as she burped the child, then laid him back down?

Beth's face cringed and rage caused her to grind her teeth together, as she forcefully extinguished the cigar. The Lady of The House walked over to a small wooden chest on another table and withdrew a hand filled with money.

"Now what do you believe would be a fair amount to pay," Beth calmly asked?

At first sight of the money Betty Lee rose from the chair and started walking over toward Beth. Once Betty Lee was off her sofa and slightly away from the baby, Beth withdrew a Remington 36mm handgun and shot her in the stomach, at which she dropped to the ground. The maid ran into the room and screamed at the sight of Betty Lee crouched on the floor, with blood on her hands and clothes. Beth still had the smoking weapon pointed toward Betty Lee, until she gradually placed it back into the drawer.

Baby Adam was bawling his head off after being frightened by the loud bang, therefore, Beth walked over, picked him up from the basket, cuddled him gently, and started walking from the room. Betty Lee tried to grab onto her leg but was too weak to interfere, thus, Beth paid her no attention and went by.

"You bitch," Betty Lee stated!

"She came here and sold me Jonathan's baby and left town… Get those Mexicans to come get rid of her body, and make sure they completely understand what happened," Beth instructed!

"Yes Mrs. Becket! Right away ma'am," answered the maid as she ran to fetch the Mexicans!

"Oh, come with your new mommy! Let us go outside and get some fresh air. I'll tell you all about how them Cherokees murdered your daddy! After all, we can not have them get away with murder, now can we," Beth declared!?

With Baby Adam cuddled against her chest Beth walked out onto her verandah, where she strolled about while relating her version of what happened to her belated husband. Betty Lee laid helplessly on the floor until both women left the room, then crawled towards the table where Beth placed the handgun. She had lost a lot of blood and the trail of red stain stretched from where she had gotten shot, but she was determined to seek justice. With her last ounce of strength Betty Lee reached up onto the table and knocked everything aside, as she retrieved the handgun. The wounded female held onto pieces of furniture and willed herself toward the front door. The entrance was open, and Betty Lee could hear Beth outside with her child, however, she fell dead before she could reach the doorframe. Beth stood out on the verandah cuddling Baby Adam, who reminded her of her deceased son Horace Becket.

The End

The
StreetAuthor

CPSIA information can be obtained
at www.ICGtesting.com
Printed in the USA
LVHW052158100621
689925LV00015B/614